COVERT MANIPULATION:

An Introducing Psychology Guide for Beginners – How to Perform Mind Control to Win Friends, to Analyze & Influence People Learning Persuasion Techniques & Reading Body Language

By: David Drive

Copyright © 2019 – David Drive
All rights reserved

The content contained within this book may not be reproduced, duplicated or transmitted without direct written permission from the author or the publisher.
Under no circumstances will any blame or legal responsibility be held against the publisher, or author, for any damages, reparation, or monetary loss due to the information contained within this book. Either directly or indirectly.

Legal Notice:
This book is copyright protected. This book is only for personal use. You cannot amend, distribute, sell, use, quote or paraphrase any part, or the content within this book, without the consent of the author or publisher.

Disclaimer Notice:
Please note the information contained within this document is for educational and entertainment purposes only. All effort has been executed to present accurate, up to date, and reliable, complete information. No warranties of any kind are declared or implied. Readers acknowledge that the author is not engaging in the rendering of legal, financial, medical or professional advice. The content within this book has been derived from various sources. Please consult a licensed professional before attempting any techniques outlined in this book.

By reading this document, the reader agrees that under no circumstances is the author responsible for any losses, direct or indirect, which are incurred as a result of the use of information contained within this document, including, but not limited to errors, omissions, or inaccuracies.

Table of Contents

Introduction 1
Chapter 1: What is Manipulation 4
  Why People Manipulate 6
  Mental Health Effect of Manipulation 7
  Manipulation in Relationships 8
  Examples of Manipulative Behavior 10
    Not giving the entire account 11
    Lying 11
    Devaluation and love-bombing 11
    Constant mood swings 12
    Denial 12
    Punishment 12
    Minimizing 12
    Targeting the victim 13
    Diversion 13
    Guilt-tripping 13
    Flattery 13
    Excessive aggression 14
  Emotional and Psychological Effects of Manipulation 14
    Short-Term Effects 15
    Long-Term Effects 16
  Common Traits of Victims 18
  How to Deal With Manipulation 19
Chapter 2: Mind Control and Brainwashing 22
  Brainwashing 24
  How People Can Brainwash You 26
    Isolation 26
    Confrontations on self-esteem 27
    Us vs. Them 27
    Blind obedience 28
    Testing 29
  How Others Use Mind Control Against You 30
    Isolation 31

    Moody behavior..31
    Metacommunication..31
    Neuro-linguistic programming............................32
    Uncompromising rules..32
  How to Prevent Mind Control 33
  Gain Control over Any Situation 35
    Don't do whatever you feel compelled to do..............35
    Don't let the dynamite explode before you put it out ..36
    Be an action taker 36

Chapter 3: Mind Games and Mind Games Relationships 38
  What Are Mind Games Relationships? 41
    Playing hard to get 41
    Projecting...41
    Sending varied messages 42
    Guilt-tripping 42
    Withholding affection 42
  Playing Mind Games in Relationships 43
    Twisting the facts 43
    Dismissing and deflecting 44
    Subtle erosion of confidence............................45
  Is Mind Games Normal in a Relationship? 45
  Why People Play Mind Game? 48
    To manipulate..49
    They enjoy the rush..49
    Test the water 50
  How to Deal With Mind Games in Relationships 51
    Having strong personal boundaries.........................51
    Seek advice from a trusted person 52
    Call your partner on their behavior........................52
    Never attempt to change the player 52
    Move on from such person 53

Chapter 4: Persuasion, Types of Persuasion, and Power of Persuasion 54
  How Persuasion Differs Today....................................57
    A tremendous increase in persuasive messages.........57
    Persuasive communication spreads far more quickly...58

- Persuasion is a big business 58
- Subtle form in modern persuasion 58
- Complexity of persuasion 58
- Various Types of Persuasion 59
  - Appeal-to-reason 59
  - Appeal-to-emotion 60
  - Body language 61
  - Communication skills.. 61
  - Sales techniques... 61
  - Personality tests 62
- The Power of Persuasion 62
- Persuasion: The Heartbeat of Economy 63
- Boosting Your Power of Persuasion 66
  - Be smart about figures 66
  - Leading people to self-discovery............................ 67
  - Repeat, then repeat and then repeat..................... 67
  - Using Monroe's motivated sequence 67
- The Difference between Manipulation and Persuasion ... 69
  - The rise of vulnerability 71

Chapter 5: Body Language and Nonverbal Communication... 73
- Understanding Body Language and Facial Expressions .. 74
  - Facial expression 75
  - The eyes 77
  - The mouth... 79
  - Gestures 80
  - The arms and legs 82
  - Posture 83
  - Personal space 84
  - Personal distance – 1.5 to 4 feet 85
  - Social distance – 4 to 12 feet................................. 85
  - Public distance – 12 to 25 feet............................... 86
- The Role of Body Language in Communication............. 86
  - Regulating 87
  - Substituting 87
  - Conflicting 88
  - Accenting/moderating 88

    Complementing 88
    Repeating 89
Chapter 6: How to Read Body Language and Basic Science to comprehend it.. 90
    Become Observant 92
        Body language in a cluster 94
        Keep it simple... 95
        Reading body language in its context 97
    Scientific Body Language Secrets That Will Make You More Successful 98
        Use the power of touch when you want to be more earnest.. 99
        Lie down when you want to be more creative and innovative 100
        Flex muscle if you want to have better determination and willpower 100
        Cross your arms if you desire to feel more persistent and determined.. 101
        Make your best impression of Superman when you want to have more confident 101
        Smile if you want to bring down stress................... 102
        Tilt your head forward if you want to make people, and even yourself, feel more comfortable 103
        Mimic their nonverbal expressions if you want to understand better someone else's feelings.............. 103
        Stand at an angle if you want to resolve an interpersonal difference 104
        Use your hands if you need to enhance information retention 105
        Chew gum if you want to feel more upbeat and happier 105
Chapter 7: A Comprehensive Look at Covert Emotional Manipulation 106
    A Deeper Look at Manipulation Tactics 111
    Covert Manipulation Victims Mistake Interest for Regard 116
        Learning the hard way about genuine regard 117

    Genuine love – unrestricted positive regard 118
  The Route to Self-Empowerment 118

Chapter 8: Secret Codes of Psychological and Emotional Manipulation 121

  Decoding the Emotional and Psychological and Manipulation 123
    Advantage of home 124
    Looking for weakness and confirming your baseline by allowing you to speak first 124
    Manipulation of facts 125
    Overwhelm victims with statistics and facts 125
    Overwhelm victims with red tape and procedures 126
    Exhibiting negative emotions by raising voice 126
    Negative surprises 126
    Giving you little or no time to make decision 127
    Poking at your weakness and disapprove you through the use of cynical humor 127
    Criticize and judge you to make you feel incompetent always 128
    The silent treatment 128
    Pretend ignorance 128
    Guilt-baiting 129
    Victimhood 129
  Control: The Power behind Psychological and Emotional Manipulation 130
    To keep track of you 133
    To make friends with you when it is suitable for them 134
    To micromanage you 134
    To "mirror" you as if you're a child 135
  How Manipulators Use Language to Dominate 136

Chapter 9: Emotional Manipulation Tactics Manipulators Use to Win and Confuse You 139

  Manipulator's Ambitions 140
    Lying 141
    Denial 142
    Avoidance 142

Guilt, shame, and blame 143
Intimidation 147
Playing the victim 147
Nonsensical conversations from hell 148
Generalizations and blanket statements 149
Conscious misrepresenting of feelings and thoughts to the level of absurdity 151

Chapter 10: How to Tell if You Are Being Emotionally Manipulated 154
What Do Manipulative People Do Best? 160

Chapter 11: Winning Friends and Influencing Others with These Tactics to Enhance Self-Esteem 164
Setting a stimulating pattern 165
   Value people 165
   Project confidence 166
   A touch of drama isn't bad 166
The Art of Winning People 167
   Sincere appreciation 167
   Indirect call of attention to mistakes 168
   Talk about your mistakes as well 168
   Never give orders 169
   Let the other person save face 169
   Praise every little improvement 170
   Give people an excellent reputation 170
   Use encouragement 170
   Make others happy about your suggestions 171
Ignite the Art of Reading People through Your Super Senses 171
   Examine cues of body language 172
   Read facial expression 174
   Take note to your intuition 174
   Discern emotional power 176
   Be aware of the presence of people 176
   Watch people's eyes 177
   Observe the feel of a hug, handshake, or touch 177
   Listen to the tone of laugh and voice 178

Conclusion 179

Introduction

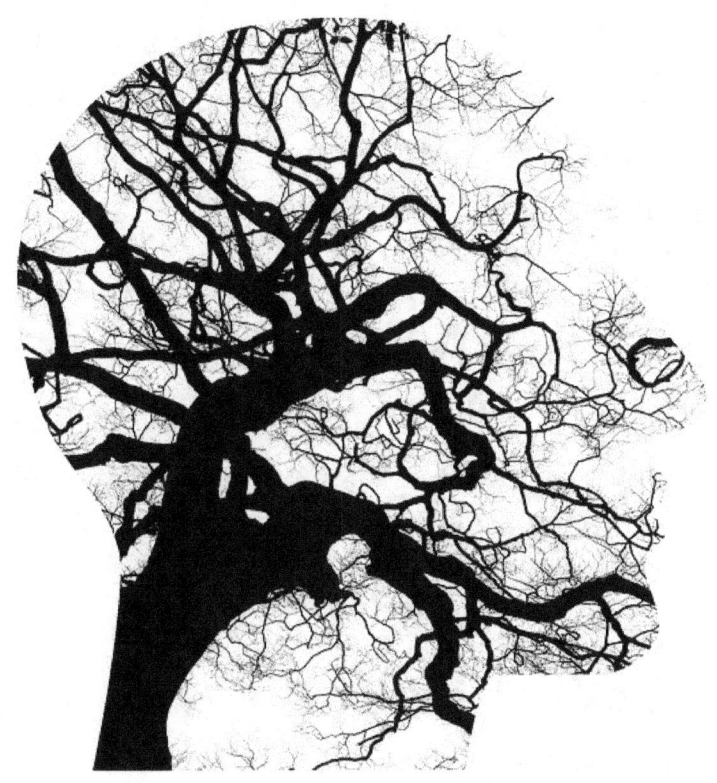

Congratulations on choosing *Covert Manipulation: An Introducing Psychology Guide for Beginners.*

Every day, almost everyone engages in the act of manipulation, and downloading this book is a good step into having a clear understanding of the world of manipulation. Usually, it is difficult for you to know if someone is manipulating you since manipulators use various tactics to conceal their evil actions. In this book, you will see multiple examples of manipulation and how manipulators use their tactics to win and confuse their victims. Ultimately, this book takes a step further to analyze languages manipulators use and how you can catch them in their games.

To this end, some of the chapters in this book will discuss mind games, mind control, and brainwashing. These are some of the weapons manipulators used to control their victims. The book shows the manners in which manipulators use them, what everyone needs to watch out for, and also how not to fall into their traps. Reading about these tactics is one thing, but having a glimpse into some practical examples is another. And this is where some of the chapters in this book become quite useful. You will learn from different models and come away to have a firm grasp as to what to watch out for, so you don't fall a victim.

With a clear perception of these tactics out of the way, this book will discuss some ways you can win friends and also influence people with some simple yet powerful practical examples. It will go deeper into the art of winning people to your side and how you can ignite your super senses through the art of reading people.

There are several books on Covert Manipulation on the shelves; we will like to appreciate you again for making this one your choice! We are making all the possibilities to be sure that this book has all the necessary and practical information you need to thrive. Thank you once again!

Chapter 1: What is Manipulation

Manipulation is when you ignore feelings of others, and at the same time, harms their desire to get what you want, similar to applying indirect tactics to control behavior, relationships, and emotions. Manipulators operate by using persuasion, charm, coax, misdirection, and trickery. Fooling people to force them to give them what they want is the underlying idea of every manipulation. Even when caught up in their scheme, manipulators tend to imagine they are doing their victim a favor.

When you are not listening to others, disregard their desires, or pretend as if your desires cost nobody else a price, you may find yourself falling into this behavior. And what about external signs? The presence of a manipulator has a strain, tension, conflicts, and complaints to a situation. Some utilize passive manipulations, employing a 'poor me' scenarios to entice pity and sympathy out of people. For other manipulators, their scheme is laying subtle guilt trips to make others think that what they want is wrong.

For people that engage in periodic manipulation, they tend to tell an acquaintance they feel 'fine' when they are depressed. Technically, this is a form of manipulation since it controls their partner's perceptions of and reactions to them.

Particularly in intimate relationships, there is a connection with emotional abuse with some of the insidious consequences of manipulation. When it harms the physical, mental, and emotional health of the victims of manipulation, most people have a negative perception of manipulation.

Manipulation is not close to being a healthy behavior, though an impulse that most times stems from profound anxiety and fear, manipulators engage in the act since they desire to control anyone or anything around them. People may find it difficult to bond with their genuine self when they engage in manipulation and others that experience manipulation can go through various poor health.

Why People Manipulate

There are several reasons why people choose to manipulate others. These reasons can vary based on the individual. For some people, they engage in manipulation at times. However, others that primarily interact with manipulation often share some characteristics among themselves. Some of these traits include:

- Fear of being abandoned

- Feelings of hopelessness, helplessness, or worthiness

- Need to raise self-esteem

- Need for control and power over others

- Willingness to put their emotions over the well-being of others

Mental Health Effect of Manipulation

When people overlook it, manipulation can result in weak mental health consequences for the people who encounter manipulation. In an intimate relationship, constant manipulation can also lead to emotional abuse taking place, which in some cases, can have a similar effect to trauma, especially when the victim of manipulation is made to feel ashamed or guilty.

Victims of chronic manipulation may:

- Have depression

- Develop anxiety

- Develop unhealthy coping patterns

- Regularly attempting to please the manipulative partner

- Lie about their feelings

- Put the needs of another person before theirs

- Find it hard to trust others

In some situations, the height of manipulation can be so pervasive that the victim may question their perception of reality. A perfect example is the classic movie *Gaslight*, where the husband of a woman subtly manipulates her until she no longer trusts her opinions.

Manipulation in Relationships

In close relationships such as those between friends, family members, and romantic partners, long-term manipulation can have severe effects. Through manipulation, the health of a relationship can deteriorate, leading to the poor mental health of those in the affair or perhaps the termination of the relationship.

In partnership or marriage, manipulation can make a spouse to feel isolated, bullied, or unworthy. Even in healthy relationships, a partner can unconsciously manipulate the other to avoid confrontation or even in an attempt to keep their partner from feeling burdened. Some individuals may even know they are being manipulated in their relationship and choose to downplay or overlook it. In a close relationship, manipulation can take various shapes, including guilt, exaggeration, selectively showing affection or gift-giving, passive aggression, and secret-keeping.

For some parents that manipulate their children, they are setting them up for depression, guilt, eating issues, anxiety, and other mental health issues. In a study, parents who continuously use manipulation tactics on their children may strengthen the possibility of their children using manipulative behavior.

Hints of manipulation in the parent-child relationship may consist of downplaying the achievements of a child, lack of accountability from a parent, making the child feel culpable, and a necessity for the parent to involve themselves with various phases of the child's life. Also, others can feel someone manipulates them when they are in a toxic friendship.

Manipulative friendship is when an individual uses the other person to achieve their desires without any care of their friend's feelings. Such manipulative friend will use coercion or guilt to extort approvals, including getting loans, or reaching out to that friend during emotional needs and tend to find an excuse when their friend has requests from them.

Examples of Manipulative Behavior

Occasionally, people may manipulate others without having any knowledge of their deed, while some may actively make an effort to fortify their manipulative tactics. Here are some examples of manipulative behaviors:

- Implicit threats
- Withholding information
- Dishonesty
- Gaslighting
- Isolating someone from their close friends and family members
- Passive-aggressive behavior
- Using sex to achieve goals
- Verbal abuse

Also, manipulators use several tactics to control their victims. Most times, however, they target specific characters. Doing so will make it easy for them to manipulate such individual, and particular vulnerability in someone can lead them to manipulation. It may be possible for someone to become an easy mark of manipulator if they are naïve, lack an assertive native, have little confidence, easy to please, and have no confidence in themselves.

Some of the common techniques manipulators use includes:

Not giving the entire account

This scenario is far from being economical with the truth as a manipulator will always hold a crucial part of the narrative to themselves to place their target at a difficult spot.

Lying

On practically anything in their life, manipulators are always lying. They engage in this act to confuse their victim and wrong-foot them. Since they have no qualms about it, lying is one of the techniques manipulators use.

Devaluation and love-bombing

One of the manipulation tactics of the narcissists is love bombing. Manipulators use this technique to operate on a charm offensive, prevail on their victim, and hook them into thinking that the relationship is the best. Then, they will drop them like a pack of dirty cards without reason.

Constant mood swings

One handy tool of the manipulator is when their partner never knows what mood they are going to be when they get home and trying to figure out whether they will be happy or angry. This condition keeps their victim off balance and makes them more malleable.

Denial

Most times, the secure method a manipulator will use to carry out their work on their victim is by denying the offense their target accused them of ever happening.

Punishment

Manipulation can include anything from shouting, nagging, physical violence, silent treatment, and mental abuse.

Minimizing

Most times, manipulators shift the blame on their victim for overreacting by trying to gloss over their deeds as not damaging or critical, thus, turning the guilt of overplaying the issue on their victims.

Targeting the victim

Sometimes, the manipulator puts accusations on their victims for the offense. Manipulators are making their prey defend themselves while they have the upper hand of covering up their manipulation techniques. Consequently, the concentration is not on the accuser, but on the victim.

Diversion

Typical way manipulators take on their victims is to divert the discussion away from their acts and move the dialogue onto a separate matter.

Guilt-tripping

Most times, a manipulator will guilt-trip their partner by telling their victim that they are selfish and doesn't care about them or their life is easy. Doing so will aid confusion and anxiety for their victim.

Flattery

A usual manipulator will use praise, charm, or smooth-talk the partner to gain the trust of that person. Logically, the victim is glad to get such respects. However, by doing so, they unconsciously lower their guard.

Excessive aggression

Most times, manipulators make use of aggression and rage to appall their target to admit defeat.

Also, the anger is a device to extinguish any further discussion on the matter as the victim is nervous, nevertheless concentrated by now on holding back the annoyance instead of the original issue.

Emotional and Psychological Effects of Manipulation

It is most likely for people to see the effects when someone sexually or physically abuses another person. However, this case is not the same when it comes to mental and emotional abuse. The scars are not physical, but they can affect the abused person for the rest of their life, particularly for those that refuse to seek help from a professional. Ultimately, mental manipulation can result in problems with trust, intimacy, security, and respect. There are long and short term effects when it comes to emotional manipulation which we treat below.

Short-Term Effects

1. Confusion and surprise – feeling like whatever is happening cannot possibly right as the victim wonders why the person that has been a friend or loved one is now acting like a stranger.

2. Self-questioning – the victim may wonder if they quite remember things right or if something is wrong with them. This situation is the consequence of the manipulators questioning everything the victim does, or the manipulators telling them that they have the wrong perspectives, and the manipulative party is right.

3. Vigilance and anxiety – for the victim to prevent the future case of manipulation, they may become hyper-vigilant toward themselves and perhaps others. They will attempt to avoid behaviors that might rock the boat, or looking for a reaction in other people that point toward an outburst.

4. Being passive – since taking action may lead to more pain in an emotionally abusive relationship, being passive can become the default. This case is something that can be

difficult to do when the victim is in a situation as stressful as they can be.

5. Guilt and shame – the victim may blame themselves or find themselves feeling guilty of setting off the manipulative presence in their life.

6. Avoid eye contact – when someone has gone through manipulation, such individual may end up avoiding eye contact and becoming smaller inside of themselves to take up less space and feel less likely to be picked on by the manipulator.

7. Walking on eggshells – when one doesn't know what will cause a spike in behavior from the other person, the situation can lead to overthinking about every little thing the other person does to ensure one doesn't upset or anger the manipulator.

Long-Term Effects

1. Numbness and isolation – the victim becomes an observer rather than someone who acts, feeling little to nothing at all, even in cases which should make them joyful. As a result, they

feel hopeless and damaged, unable to ever feel emotions again.

2. In need of approval – this situation manifests in manners like excessive accomplishing, being kind to all and sundry, being a people pleaser, and paying too much attention to appearance. After feeling like they were not enough for an extended period, their instinct is to make themselves appear perfect so others will appreciate them.

3. Feeling resentful – this case can appear as frustration, impatience, irritability, and blame. Resentment inevitably requires release, but this can be difficult to seek and allow. After a person has experienced forceful manipulation, it can be hard to see anything but that bad behavior.

4. Excessive judging – the victim of manipulation may find themselves watching for what others are doing and holding people and even themselves, to quite high standards. It is a device of feeling in control after not being in control. Most times, this situation requires time and self-compassion to move past.

5. Anxiety and depressive disorder – following a circumstance of manipulation or other emotional abuse, manipulators have told the victim many lies that they often believe them. However, the good news is that the victims can mend the situation over time.

Common Traits of Victims

Even though a skilled manipulator employs emotional manipulation on almost anyone, they look for some common themes. Common victim types are people that attach their self-worth to meeting the needs of others. This type of individual draws manipulators to them since they are easy to manipulate, blame, and victimize. It will be quite easy for this type of person to succumb to abuse since they need to meet the needs of others to feel loved.

Also, those who have a problematic sense of rejecting something from other people are the usual type for manipulators to prey. By trying to avoid conflict, manipulators may take that advantage to do what they want without worrying about any repercussions.

Individuals who find it hard to express negative emotions will typically avoid confrontation and keep things happy, no matter the situation. With that, manipulators sometimes search for these people since threats may be all that is required to get whatever it is they want.

People with a weak sense of self mostly have it hard to distinguish themselves from the abuser. Such a condition as this makes it difficult to trust their feelings or make decisions that will make them happy. Manipulators appreciate that because they don't need to try as hard to get what they are after.

How to Deal With Manipulation

You have read from the above ways to interact with a manipulative person, but there are things you can do yourself to raise your self-esteem as well. You will be glad to know that when you have higher self-confidence, it will help you fight against a manipulator before they can damage your overall well-being. Follow these guidelines and tips if you are trying to get yourself out of a manipulative relationship or environment.

- Identify and be aware of things that are going on around you. You can go back to read some of the points above, so you know how to catch any manipulator the next time around. Have in-depth knowledge about how manipulation works and where it leads.

- Inculcate a listening habit to yourself and your feelings. In any event of confusion and self-doubting, take serious cognizance of that situation and why you are feeling that way. Pay attention to what the manipulative person is saying or doing and how such actions affect you.

- Give more thought to actions than words. Never assume that when an individual says something, it is the truth or you need to act upon it. Pay more attention to what someone does instead and base your feelings on that.

- Be aware that you are not a problem. In case you have discovered that someone has manipulated you, understand that it is not your fault. Know that you did nothing wrong to cause it and the other person has their problems. Don't allow this situation, however, to lead to sympathy, keep it on an awareness level.

- Be assertive for yourself. You can begin by choosing to stop responding to methods in the manner you did before. Learn to say no and speak out if you want, and their reaction is not your responsibility.

- Ponder over having an affair with someone else. Choose if you wish to speak with friends about how you feel or perhaps confront the person. In any way, consider all the options and do what is comfortable for you.

- By confronting any manipulator, you are taking back your power. However, do this if you do not believe you are in harm's way. In other words, you are not doing anything wrong when you explain how you feel and what is bothering you. Demand that the other person changes their behaviors and never allow them to continue with the same routine. Do what you need to do and take back your power.

Chapter 2: Mind Control and Brainwashing

Distant strangers that have no inch of your best interest at heart may be controlling your mind. If this appears like a paranoid fantasy, brace yourself and read on.

The definition of mind control is manipulation, brainwashing, and coercive persuasion, thought reform, coercive control, mental control, and many more. While there are various names for mind control is an indication of a shortage of harmony which leads to distortion and confusion, particularly by people who exploit it in a hidden way for their benefit.

Thus, we conclude that mind control comes under the parasol of influence and persuasion – how to transform the behaviors and beliefs of people.

Some people may disagree that the whole thing is manipulation. In expressing this, however, we have lost essential peculiarities. Thinking of influence as a continuity will be much more useful. At one side, there are respectful and ethical influences which revere people and their rights. While on the other extreme have devastating impacts which bare people of their independence, identity, and capability to think logically and critically.

Therefore, what is mind control?

The best way to define mind control is to look at it as a scheme of influences that considerably disrupts someone of their identity or their very core, which are their beliefs, decisions, preferences, relationships, values, choice, behaviors, and so on, to create a pseudo personality or new pseudo-identity.

In the word of Philip Zimbardo, the psychologist, control is a method whereby agents or agencies distort or modify motivation, perception, or affect an individual or collective freedom of choice and action and as he suggests, everyone is vulnerable to the situation above.

The dynamics of mind control is not some obsolete secrecy that a select few know. Instead, it is a combination of group pressures and words, wrapped up in a manner that it gives a manipulator the power to craft reliance in their cohorts, making their choices for them even as allow them to believe that they are free and can make their decisions themselves. Ultimately, the mind control victim is not conscious of the changes that happen within them, nor the influence procedure.

Brainwashing

It may not be appropriate to imagine that brainwashing is about government representatives becoming reluctant spies against their countries, or head of a group applying mind control to manipulate their cohorts. You can even go further to imagine that brainwashing has a connection with misinformation distributed during the First and Second World Wars to influence large amounts of people.

However, what is brainwashing and whether we must restrict it to the earlier period?

In the 1950s, during the Korean War, some people invented the term brainwashing. They used it to give details of the way autocratic administrations had the capability of thoroughly indoctrinating American soldiers using the process of propaganda and torture.

Brainwashing is the premise of replacing the ideas, core beliefs, values, and affiliations of someone so much that such an individual has no independence over their affairs and find it difficult to think independently or critically.

So, can anyone brainwash you?

In the movie '*The Manchurian Candidate*,' during the war, the Korean soldiers captured a prosperous senator. Then, they use the power of brainwashing on the senator to work for them so they can succeed in eliminating the presidential candidate.

The movie depicts that even anyone can brainwash a powerful and intelligent person such as the senator. When you are susceptible to some extent, and you are vulnerable in your ways of thinking, some people can likely brainwash you. This case could include some that have:

- To live on the street through force, particularly young people

- Are suffering from an illness they cannot accept

- Lost their loved one through death or divorce

- They have made redundant and sacked from their job

How People Can Brainwash You

Someone who attempts to brainwash you will take a step further to be familiar with everything about you for them to manipulate your way of life. Their mission will include knowing your strengths and weakness, those you trust or are essential to you, and those that give you advice.

From that point, they will engage you with the course of brainwashing you, and they will naturally take these steps:

1. Us vs. Them
2. Isolation
3. Confrontations on self-esteem
4. Blind obedience
5. Testing

Isolation

This stage is the commencement of the brainwashing process since it is dangerous to them for you to be around your family and friends. A brainwasher dreads a situation where another opinion of someone to theirs is probing what the brainwasher is now asking to accept as real. The process of isolation begins in the process of giving you no access to friends and family or regularly checking where you are and who is with you.

Confrontations on self-esteem

When someone chooses to brainwash another, it can only be possible when the victim has low self-confidence and is in a vulnerable state. A broken individual is much cushier to recreate with the beliefs of a brainwasher.

Therefore, the brainwasher must decompose the self-esteem of the victim. They can achieve this through physical or verbal abuse, sleep deprivation, intimidation, or embarrassment. From there, a brainwasher starts to control all aspects of the victim's life, from food, using the bathroom, and even the time they sleep.

Us vs. Them

For the brainwasher to break down and remold their victim in a distinctive image, they will introduce a free lifestyle which is quite more delightful than their current way of living. The brainwasher achieves this when their target only mix with others that they have already brainwashed and as a result, will worship the latest system. Or the brainwasher could make their victims wear similar dresses, other unbending regulations that support a team dynamic, or have a set diet.

By nature, several pieces of evidence propose that humans are tribal and desire to belong to a group. Therefore, the brainwasher must influence their victim that they are part of an elite group of which is the desire of everyone. Even the brainwashers might give a new name to their victim, as in the case of abducted Patty Hearst, and soon after, her kidnappers named her Tania who eventually, after they have brainwashed her, backed with her captors.

Blind obedience

Blind obedience is the ultimate objective of every brainwasher, where they give orders, and the victim follows them without looking back. The brainwasher achieves this feat when they positively reward their victim when they make them happy, and when the victims do not, they negatively punish the person.

Also, reciting a phrase repeatedly is an excellent technique brainwashers use to control someone. Though the repeated phrase might not be a way of soothing the brain, research reveals that the 'repetitive' and the 'analytical' components of the brain are not identical. What this analysis tells us is that the mind can only perform one or the other, as such, an excellent way to prevent those skeptical thoughts is through chanting.

Testing

It will never occur to the brainwasher that they have ultimately captured their victim since there are certain situations where the person begins to recover from their autonomy and begin to have their own opinions. Not only is testing their victims indicates that they are still under their spells, but it allows the brainwashers to see the extent of the control they still have on their victims. A few aspects of tests could include carrying out a criminal act like burglarizing a home or robbing a store.

Brainwashing is real and present in many forms of today's society, not just the stuff of fantasy or imagination. Here are a few things you can do to prevent yourself not to be a victim of brainwashing:

- Don't believe the hype

- Don't follow the crowd

- Don't accept everything you read
- Look out for subliminal messages
- Don't yield to tactics of scare or fear
- Be wary of the agenda of someone
- Keep to your dreams and visions
- Don't be scared to be different
- Pay attention to your instinct
- Do your research

How Others Use Mind Control Against You

Mind control is a concept by which an external force controls the actions and thoughts of a subject. They achieve this through physical or psychological means, and most times involves breaking down the person so they can gain complete control.

You may be thinking that all this appears entirely implausible and far-fetched, you may want to believe that people engage in mind control in our everyday lives, from media bias in politics to advertising products.

Furthermore, you may want to read about these ways someone can use mind control against you:

Isolation

When you discover that someone or a situation is gradually isolating you from your family and friends, then, it is likely an indication that someone is attempting to control your mind. No doubt your loved ones will complain to you about some unusual behaviors with your new friend, but they want to run away from this situation happening. For them to break your spirit, they need you to be vulnerable and alone.

Moody behavior

Be careful in a situation where your partner sulks when they don't get their way. And do you try to routine your behavior to prevent or stop an argument? Such a situation as this may be the beginning of mind control, where you are changing your actions due to the behavior or reaction of someone else. It is a sign of tell-tale that those people are attempting to control your mind and are indeed getting the upper hand.

Metacommunication

Metacommunication is a method whereby someone gives subtle hints and clues with the use of nonverbal cues. An excellent instance is when a woman gets a call from her partner, asking her if she is okay and shrugging her shoulders, she responds by saying yes with a sign. This situation is a clear indication that she is far from being okay, yet her verbal response is affirmative. Some people employ metacommunication to establish subliminal opinions.

Neuro-linguistic programming

NLP or neuro-linguistic programming is a method of layering specific feelings with the use of words into the unconscious mind of someone without the person being aware of their actions.

NLP assesses various features of an individual and uses verbal communication to plant ideas. For example, when someone can adjust to a situation through visual patterns, they will speak to that person with languages that use visual clues like 'can you *see* what I mean?' For someone familiar with auditory cues, they will result in using the hearing language used on them, such as 'Can you *hear* me clearly.'

Uncompromising rules

Does your spouse put irrational rules on your way of living? In case your partner blocks all access to your friends or money, expects you to meet impossible deadlines, regulated bathroom breaks, and mealtimes, then, mind control is happening.

This process implies that they deny you of making your own decisions so that you adhere to a precise set of behaviors. Consequently, you stop having your thoughts, and this circumstance makes it easier for them to instill their secret plans.

How to Prevent Mind Control

If you experience any of the above instances and you can recognize them, then it may be time for you to disentangle yourself from that person and their effort to control your mind.

The first step you need to take is staying close in contact with family and friends. Prevent your new friend from getting in the way of your connecting with some of your family members or old friends. Maintain your ground to make contact with them, and you're still getting 'no' for an answer, then walk away.

Never accommodate irritable and moody behavior. Deal with it in a disdain manner that it deserves. Try to inform your partner that their behavior is childish and immature, and you won't put up with it.

Also, pay careful attention to nonverbal clues that do not correlate with what someone is saying. Probe them if their responses do not complement their actions or body language.

It may be a bit hard to spot NLP since anyone using it will possibly be a professional. However, signs you need to watch are new sensations that you have met your ideal companion, or that the individual you have just found is your perfect match. Be careful of a person who uses blurred expressions that make no sense or keeps mirroring your body language.

Finally, watch out for uncompromising rules. Seek out for advice from family and close friends when someone imposes inflexible regulations on you. Indeed, they would have exhausted you with low self-confidence by the time the situation gets to this point.

When you inform your family and friends, their immediate response to your condition should be enough to release you from this dreadful deception.

Gain Control over Any Situation

Don't be like some people whose lifestyle is typical of passengers in an unrestrained and uncontrollable vehicle. Instead of taking charge to control the situation by taking the driver's seat, these people operate the vehicle as commuters. They try to have power over what is out of their influence instead of what is within it.

When things appear as if you have no control over them, with these examples below, you can gain control over any situation:

Don't do whatever you feel compelled to do

The more powerfully the circumstance drives you to take instant action, the more likely you shouldn't. When the pull is intense, it may be you have activated your fight-or-flight physiology. That is excellent, especially when you're facing a life-or-death situation and need to react instantly. In most of life's circumstances, it serves you better to reflect before you respond.

Don't let the dynamite explode before you put it out

Sometimes, you may find yourself in dangerous conditions and shrink from facing others, whether family, friends, or colleagues. It can be an enormous blunder you make at the office that can keep the company at a loss, or perhaps you make a poor judgment that hurts a companion. Logically, you will want to avoid these situations since avoiding them will avert any conflict. However, this tactic may unconsciously grind you down, resulting in anxiety and chronic stress. Rather than doing that, face the situation. Instead of dealing with it passively, assume responsibility, and set off the conversation with a high level of confidence. Learn to understand that you have control over how you say what you say and the consequences that might result from it.

Be an action taker

Try to do something instead of feeling helpless and victimized, particularly when it comes to business settings. Most times, employers tend to cheat people when they don't get the bonus they were counting on or perhaps the employer dismisses them. Instead of stewing in frustration, imagine the realistic actions you could take to defend yourself and strive for more substance for yourself. Think of how you can be in charge of your work performance, your rapport with your boss, and whether you are working at upgrading your education out of your occupation to enhance your marketability and skills. In case you are out of a job before now, you can maintain your structure and be in command of your daily schedule. Wake up the usual time every day, clean up, and dress to the nines, and never detach yourself from your routine. Take a step further to read job placements and submit applications for as many vacancies as possible, exchange ideas with social groups in your field of relevance, or gain new knowledge that will advance you to a more privileged position.

For various situations in life, perception is crucial, and it starts with your mind. As a result, the next time you're in a position where you think you have no power, take a bit of time to adjust your thoughts. It will surprise you to realize how you can transform from feeling powerless to powerful.

Chapter 3: Mind Games and Mind Games Relationships

In a circumstance where there is no coherence in someone's words and actions, and their words do not correlate with their past words, then, mind game is indeed taking place. Mind games force the victim to doubt their thinking or reasoning ability and intuition. The purpose for the person playing mind games is to make you rely on them to make your choices for you since it is hard for you to trust your ability to make the best decisions for yourself.

Many motives make people play mind games, just in various ways people live through them. It is crucial to watch out for people that play the mind game and also essential to understand the background in which such individual plays. At length, your reaction to these tactics is vital for you to be familiar with how to tackle those games in the future.

In the first place, you must have clear farsightedness that the intention of a co-worker or colleague that plays a mind game is quite not the same with your family member or friend playing a mind game. Discovering the complicated characteristics of mind games will better prepare you to tackle the most illogical reason and extremely complex for such games.

Acquire, safeguard or get control

The significant rationale of people playing mind games is to acquire, gain, and preserve control. When they have the power to move you to do what they want or elicit a specific response from you, then they get the powerful feeling that they are in control of how you live and also the entire situation.

In case you experience insignificant and perhaps no control at your job, it may be their method of making up for the loss of domination at the office by taking back that feeling with you. Essentially, on the part of the person playing the mind game, it is a matter of insecurity. At this level, it is your responsibility to look inside and find out whether you are sacrificing control for a particular goal, inclusive of purposely fulfilling the necessity of the person playing the mind game, or someone is unsuspectingly coercing, manipulating, and controlling you.

Also, resentment may be the harbinger of feelings of anxiety. When your spouse thinks they have no power over their lives or feels they are a disappointment; then, it is possible they picked you exclusively to relieve them of their frustrations and anger. Sometimes, it may be for the reason that you represent how they want to be. It could be that you display success and confidence that they wished they had, and possibly by engaging in their mind games, they may feel like the winner for a change. In any case, doesn't that make them victorious as well when they beat a confident and successful person?

What Are Mind Games Relationships?

Usually, people engage in mind games as a result of immaturity, insecurity, or possess a controlling behavior. These sets of people are not mature enough to have a lasting association. Some of the reasons for this begin from lack of confidence and their helplessness to commit and relate with others in a beneficial way. Some of the typical mind games these people engage in relationships include:

Playing hard to get

In this situation, they are trying not to exhibit their affection and interest for someone they are dating. The goal for doing this is to make them appear more critical before their partner. They abhor appearing desperate or easy and take great pleasure in the feeling of someone chasing them.

Projecting

People project when they ascribe their actions and thoughts to another person. For instance, an unfaithful individual might blame their partner for involving in immorality. Accordingly, the person they hold responsible uses their energy protecting themselves rather than controlling their emotions, breathe, and force the concentration on their partner and judging their actions.

Sending varied messages

For a while, someone who sends messages may appear interested and then, disregards you totally, only to later begin to act attracted to you again. So, what point does the person intend to make? In any case, their action can be intentional since the person is not sure of their feelings. However, when this action is deliberate, their goal then is to make you feel insecure, desperate, and have more focus on them.

Guilt-tripping

A person can make use of the guilt-trip method to weaken the personality boundaries of someone else. Most times, when someone feels guilty, they tend to let others outshine them and do awful things they wouldn't allow if self-reproach were not there in the first place.

Withholding affection

Sadly, and most often, this situation happens in relationships. Some people suppress affection if they have no control over relationships. Indeed, don't mix up this case with being mad at your spouse for a reasonable cause.

Playing Mind Games in Relationships

Any communication with someone else has the possibility of involving some mind game. Indeed, many of us are great when it comes to playing mind games in relationships. When someone uses mind games for dubious purposes is when the problems start. Devious people desire to be in power, and several of them have gained knowledge of how to turn the switches of others and get the hang of subtle emotional signals to control the other people. Since mind games include twisting the facts and manipulation, creating doubts to destabilize others becomes so handy for them.

When someone has a tumultuous childhood, they are more likely to play mind games. If a child has to deal with unreasonable and unfair parents, such a child will discover habits of manipulating the situation in a smart, passive way to handle emotions. Some of these children take these socially impaired hacking means into their relationships as grownups.

Twisting the facts

For the benefit of the manipulator's account of actions, people engage in mind games to distort the details of an event. A manipulator will perceive the circumstances their way and will usually be short of the compassion to value the opinion of someone else. It is in their custom to disregard feelings and execute their side of events again, effectively avoiding any other outlook of a situation. Such a case as this tends to be provoking for the spouse who feels misunderstood and misheard.

Dismissing and deflecting

Indeed, when someone disregards your feelings, they are playing mind games with you. They will utter something offensive, and when you respond, they will tell you that you are too sensitive. A caring, healthy individual will not enjoy upsetting other person and be careful not to repeat the situation. As for someone playing mind game, such person will make a mental observation of that weakness and hold it as ammunition they will draw on later to manipulate and control you. Other tactics they use is when you attempt to have a conversation with them about their behavior or a situation you don't like that happen. Rather than communicating or listening, someone exploiting you with mind games will sidetrack the discussion and blame their behavior on another thing you have done.

Subtle erosion of confidence

With time, someone playing mind games with you will lead you to question yourself, and such circumstance undermines confidence. Mind game players may also give comments that you are fortunate to have them as nobody will love you as they do, or you won't find someone else to love you. A player of mind game will talk down at your confidence to keep you feeling degrading rather than bringing the best in you. Consequently, leaving the relationship may never be an option for you.

Is Mind Games Normal in a Relationship?

Have you come across something like this?When you have the feeling that your spouse is undervaluing your relationship with them, tell yourself that it is all right that you are going to make yourself inaccessible this week. True to form, this tactic makes your partner desire you more with a swift turnaround that it is nearly a joke. It's more or less like playing a game, yet it works well.

Many of us adhere to this advice, in some way standardized to accept playing mind game as an active component of relationships.

Since the young age, situations taught us about coercion, debasement, charm, retaliation, emotional blackmail, silent treatment, blame, and so many more to get specific reactions from our peers and parents. And our teens saw us pushing the boundaries to distinguish how far it is likely for us to come off with what our desires.

By 18 to 25 years of age, many of us outgrow this since we have found better mechanisms to navigate the life of an adult. Sadly, however, many of us don't.

In our teens, for a lot of reasons, something put a break in the development of our emotions. We never got hold of a better tool for navigating the adult life, and to achieve our desires, we result in using the silent treatment, blame, charm, comparison, coercion, and so many more. For us, everyone is doing it, but it doesn't make it acceptable or right for a grown adult to act or think like a teen or adolescent.

There must be a distinction involving how a teen attempts to induce interest or love and how a grownup get their wants and needs met. It is possible that, once in a while, some of us relapse to some juvenile behaviors, however, in most cases, as we grow older, our tolerance for infantile behavior decreases that we imagine adults to have outgrown like whining, yelling, self-absorption, finger-pointing, tantrums, and manipulating other people because of what they want.

It may happen that a partner may be taking someone for granted. Rather than calmly asking for what you want, having a matured discussion, and negotiating what meets both of your needs, you result to making yourself less available. Quite predictably, the conversion can be so quick since the insecurities of the other person have taken over; however, only temporary. The moment they feel secure again, they start failing to appreciate you - yet.

For most individuals that have immature emotions and who imagine that healthy aspects of relationships are mind games, they apply even more mind games to get the other person to give them the attention, love, respect and so much more that they want.

Someone who loves you, devoted to you, and wants their emotions to be in parallel with yours will check out just so that they can bear your childishness for a while longer. Sadly, when the other person emotionally checks out, you engage even further mental games. But by then, the person can't take it anymore.

As for other people, they may not be so tolerant with a grownup who behaves like a child. They move on ahead of endurance any opportunity you may have to play another mind game – also, others who have zero tolerance for unintelligent mind games. To them, teaching you a lesson is the best way to get you to grow up. They allow you to play the player. And since they are fully aware of what they are doing versus you who think it's a normal part of relationships, they can indeed mess you up.

Why People Play Mind Game?

For many people, they experience frustration and confusion in dating relationships. It can be quite tough to figure out the opposite sex or hinder a deep, meaningful connection, especially when such a partner you are interested in plays mind games.

There could be several motives why people engage in mind games, and on occasion, they are so ignorant of their own needs, much less you're that they don't even know they are playing games.

People play mind games because of the following reasons:

To manipulate

Individuals engage in mind games to selfishly manipulate other people for them to accomplish their wish, such as:

- Always having a company
- Sex
- Having someone to listen to them
- A desire to control another person
- Having someone adore them
- Expecting someone to nurse their deepest wounds back to health
- Enhancing their personality since they have someone to flaunt

It may appear that not all these desires are unhealthy or wrong. It is just the way these people go about achieving their purpose that tends to be hurtful and selfish.

They enjoy the rush

Some people want to get a drift of having another person to like them. It is more or less like a challenge or a game for these people. For them, getting another person fancy them can be quite exciting.

This behavior stems from a low sense of worth and a lack of knowledge of how they upset others. Whereas others are anxious, looking for that excitement of experiencing that someone highly regards them. It is typical of a high. However, in a short period, they turn off once they realize the person they have been chasing is fond of them. All of a sudden, they have moved on to the next capture, hunting for the subsequent rush. Unfortunately, many are not aware of their actions or the reasons for them.

Test the water

Another reason the mind game players is to discover your feelings for them. Being vulnerable enough to share your deepest needs to wanting to love someone and for that person to embrace you back takes so much courage. How would you feel if you tell a person you are fond of them and they decline you in some way?

It may be that you that person lead you on, although perhaps such individual is anxious to initiate the relationship.

For so long, guys have always had the pressure of initiating a relationship. Now, it appears the table has turned as ladies are getting bolder all the time. However, both genders, deliberately or otherwise, count on the guy to make the first move and for the lady to be at the receiving end in any relationship. Remember, so many guys act macho and sturdy, but deep down, they are also nursing so much anxiety of rejection.

How to Deal With Mind Games in Relationships

Those who play mind games can be difficult to change. Meet head-on with any mind game player and let them be aware that you won't tolerate them when you notice their behavior. You should probably move on when you realize that better communication doesn't appear to solve the issue. Some other ways for you to tackle the situation include:

Having strong personal boundaries

We teach others how to behave towards us through the guidelines we establish with our bounders. Learn how to reject mind game players when it's hard to keep up with such behavior and set boundaries for them. When you know what you want and build your confidence, you will achieve firm personal boundaries.

Seek advice from a trusted person

Most times, a third person can examine the situation rationally and more wisely since they are not emotionally involved, and such people can give you unbiased and more practical guidance.

Call your partner on their behavior

A mind game player needs to know that you are conscious of what they are doing. Never make use of the same passive-aggressive techniques in an attempt to take revenge or even prevail over the game. Don't debase your confidence and tell the mind game player that you are aware of their manipulation.

Never attempt to change the player

Trying to change someone can be quite tricky, particularly a manipulative individual. If these people are manipulative and the conversation appears not enough to sort out the issue, chances are it is merely their personality and nothing much you can do about it. If you continue to try, you will be possibly messing around.

Move on from such person

In most cases, people who play mind games may not change for the better, except they are still quite at their young age. A mind game player who manipulates you or tests you is not who you need. Having a relationship with a mature individual with efficient and open communication is all that you need.

Chapter 4: Persuasion, Types of Persuasion, and Power of Persuasion

What comes to your mind when you reflect about persuasion? Do you think about a political candidate who attempts to influence voters to pick their name on the ballot box come to your mind? Or do you see the image of an advertising announcement that incites the audience to purchase a specific item? Since it has a significant influence on society as a whole, persuasion is indeed a dominant force in daily life. The power of persuasion influences legal decisions, politics, news, mass media, and advertising, and it also impacts us in turn.

Also, when you think of persuasion, you may mean something either positive or detrimental to you. An authority, such as peer pressure instructing you to do something, or you won't fit in, could be the perception of others about persuasion. It is so compelling that all of us engage in persuasion, and it is an exciting concept to discuss. At some point in our life, for some of us to accomplish a goal, we have participated in some form of persuasion. Someone has cut down on the price of an item we want to buy, or we have succeeded in getting a job through the art of persuasion.

At times, some of us take pleasure in believing that we can resist persuasion. We think that we have the power to comprehend the truth in a situation, possess a natural ability to see through the sales pitch, and with our innate skills, achieve reasonable inferences. While in some scenarios this conviction might be valid, persuasion is not just a commercial on the television tempting you to buy the most fabulous and latest product, or an over-ambitious marketer attempting to convince you to buy a car. Because of the subtlety of persuasion, the degree of our response to such influence will depend on some factors.

When we steer our thoughts toward persuasion, what often come to our minds are negative instances. However, people use persuasion as a constructive power. One such great example of persuasion in the public service campaigns geared at people to quit smoking or recycle because they use it to enhance the lives of the people.

Some of the crucial features of persuasion are that:

- Persuasion involves a deliberate attempt to influence other people; thus, it can't be accidental

- It is symbolic, applying images, words, sounds, etc

- Techniques of transmitting persuasive messages can happen in various ways such as verbally and nonverbally through radio, television, Internet, or face-to-face communication

- It is vital to have self-persuasion. People using persuasion are not coercing; instead, people can choose without reservation

- People can persuade you in different sorts of ways using different types of media

Persuasion is a symbolic process, and this process makes us try to convince other people to take out attitudes or behavior and change them into something that we want them to do.

How Persuasion Differs Today

Since the time of the Ancient Greeks, the science and art of persuasion have been of interest and how persuasion happens today or the past are the main differences. Five significant ways separate the past form of persuasion and those of the modern:

A tremendous increase in persuasive messages

If you can take a moment and think about how many advertisements you encounter every day, the figure will shock you. As some studies suggest, each day, the number of advertisements advertisers expose an average U.S. adult to ranges from 300 to more than 3,000.

Persuasive communication spreads far more quickly

The Internet, radio, and television all contribute to the rapid travel of persuasive messages.

Persuasion is a big business

Not only are establishments such as public relations companies, marketing firms, advertising agencies, and many others the only companies that rely purely on persuasive purposes, many other companies are dependent on persuasion to promote their services and sell goods.

Subtle form in modern persuasion

Indeed, you may see that the strategies of persuasion in some adverts are noticeable; however, subtle type of adverts is in some modern persuasive approach. A good example is some establishments that entice consumers to get their products or services to accomplish that estimated standard of living through cautiously crafted images.

Complexity of persuasion

Since there are varieties in consumers, they have several choices. As a result, marketers have to be savvier about choosing their persuasive message and medium.

Various Types of Persuasion

The power to convince people in a variety of ways is what several types and principles of persuasion have. While you may have to opt for the appeal-to-reason method in case you have an individual who accepts what they can hear or see since they are exceptional with fact, the technique of appeal-to-emotion will be more suited to those with a bit of belief.

First, let's go through all these methods so it can help you to understand these ranges of persuasion better and also the various impact they have on people:

Appeal-to-reason

A rational line of reasoning is what this technique makes use of with scientific method and logic being the center of the persuasion. Those who find it hard to accept arguments on the ground of faith than fact and require proof of something will be suited for appeal-to-reason. In the event of your conviction that the Earth revolves around the moon, you may need to have several facts to back up your claim if you are to convince a team of scientist to adhere to conviction. If not, persuading them to your argument will be hard.

Appeal-to-emotion

This method is not proof-based; instead, it engages arguments through emotions. Most times, because emotions can govern individuals more than their minds, appeal-to-emotion tends to be a more practical approach for the whole population. All through history, this method is factual, and there are quite a lot of examples that reveal that. For anyone to win people over to an argument, this method appeals to someone through the involvement of their imagination and faith. Also, to get people to concur with you, tradition, seduction, and even pity may come to play. Salespeople utilize the appeal-to-emotion method quite well. Through a test drive of a vehicle for people to imagine themselves in it, salespeople appeal to individuals' imagination. Apart from using seduction to entice you, many use compassion to convince people how sales have been slow, and they may want the deal. Using this form of persuasion are propaganda and advertising. Also, as a technique of getting a person to do your bidding, appealing to emotions uses tradition.

To persuade someone toward your idea and opinion, these four aids, which are:

Body language

Body language takes approximately two-third of our communication. For instance, you need to stand with your hands at your side, have a symbolic gesture of peace with your palm out, if you are looking for someone to consent to your view. It may be a sign of blocking recipient if you have your arm crossed while standing and out of their unconsciousness, they will not wish to listen to you lest dealing with you.

Communication skills

When you are good at writing and speaking skills to spread the message you want to pass out, your message will attract a lot of people. Propose a unique opportunity to them with the right product will see you appealing to them on many sides.

Sales techniques

Over time, people can learn the art of deep-rooted sales method, which is the technique exercises. What works well in sales technique is highlighting only the good points which will appeal to the needs of people and more.

Personality tests

The personality tests devices a strategy is all about the style of the interaction of someone. While some people like to speak with someone present physically, others have a preference for phone calls. Some may purchase an item only when they need it, and as for other people, they even prefer to buy products based on what they see on television. Knowing to sell an idea or a product to people comes from their personality.

The Power of Persuasion

Before reading further, you may wish to know that of all the tools you may have in your arsenal; integrity is the most important persuasion tool.

When we have a clear grasp of motivation, influence, and the theories of persuasion, we will have the control of life's driver's seat. Three simple concepts are the origin of what we desire, or will ever desire in life. You may not even be aware that less than 1 percent of the world's population can indeed apply or have a concise understanding of the twelve rules of persuasion. For that reason, as you have a glimpse into the science of persuasion and the secrets of influence, the accuracy will be complete when you have the potential of persuading and influencing. In an instant, while you accomplish your desire in life all at the same time, you will inspire others to take action as you gain influence over them. As you empower yourself with firm self-reliance, you will be able to prevail over people to your view. As you succeed with increasing your prosperity in sales and marketing, you will also turn into a captivating magnet of success.

Persuasion: The Heartbeat of Economy

In today's world, the influence of persuasion is of critical and extraordinary importance. Persuading or gaining influence of other people to our opinions is what almost all humans encounter. People are always making an effort to persuade one another with no regards to profession, age, philosophical beliefs, or religion. All of us want to have the capability to influence and persuade so other people will follow us, trust us, and listen to us. Some economists discovered in the latest study that the use of persuasion skills in the marketplace directly attributes to a massive 26 percent of gross domestic product. It is thus efficient to say that the gasoline to the economy's engine is persuasion. Since sales professionals are not liabilities to the company, but assets, to trim down on sales forces is almost impossible for any big cooperation. Even in the slowest of economies, there will be employment for first-class persuaders.

For doing something positive or negative, the skill to persuade is power. Persuasive individuals prevent wars, keep children off drugs, and enhance lives. Indeed, the influence of persuasive people has also stirred up wars, get children on drugs, and destroy lives. For the advancement and improvement of ourselves, families, friends, and communities, put a premium focus on the power of persuasion. For sure, the arts of influence and persuasion are not gifts majority of us possess since we don't have the natural gift of a persuader. Sure, we have the conventional persuaders who are naturally outgoing, social, and sometimes loud. However, the most excellent persuaders are introverts according to research.

The perception of others is that they may seem manipulative, forceful, and pushy with the notion of becoming a polished persuader. But it is dead wrong to have such an assumption. You may not achieve lasting influence from deliberate tactics, calculated maneuvers, or intimidation. Instead, you will be able to influence with the utmost integrity when you have appropriate execution of the latest persuasion strategies. Others will automatically and naturally have confidence in you and want you to persuade them since they trust you. In short, these people will be ready to do anything you tell them to do.

You must be aware that persuasion and negotiation are not the same because an indication of meeting in the middle of backing down is the meaning of negotiation. Contrary to negotiation which compromises, talking the opposite party into embracing your position and abandoning their previous stance is what an effective persuasion is all about.

Can you imagine why is it that some people, as well as some situation, can persuade us so much more than others? Your level of persuasion has a lot to do with the state in which you are. Your power of persuasion may below when you are tired or hungry or lonely or particularly needy in some other way. But understanding the psychology of persuasion is essential, perhaps even vital, for all our sakes.

Boosting Your Power of Persuasion

From podcasts to presentations, from friendly fliers to Facebook ads, from love letters to political speeches, we all have had our fair share of being on the receiving end of a tsunami of persuasive messages. In an attempt to trap our attention, people us thousands of messages to persuade us to do, think, or feel something.

Today, persuasion has turned to a household word since what we have is an increase of written opinions on the subject of persuasion. As an entrepreneur, you may be missing out on a powerful influencing tool if you haven't been paying attention to the persuasion principles other people use.

With the tips and tricks below, you can improve your influence of persuasion:

Be smart about figures

You may lose the power of persuasion when you use round figures instead of the accurate numbers when putting a value on items for sale, according to research. Never use rounded numbers when you price your services. While you are not cheating anyone with this method, you may need to be smart and prevent potential customers from asking for a discount which will reduce your actual worth.

Leading people to self-discovery

As a psychologist puts it, people usually act for their reasons, not the reasons for someone else. Don't tell people why they must change when you intend to persuade people to do something like convincing a reluctant employee to change negative behavior. Rather, help them discover their reasons for changing.

Repeat, then repeat and then repeat

Among consumers, skepticism is at an all-time high these days. For some people to believe messages about a business, they have to hear it three to five times. As you attempt to present a message that its purpose is to persuade, don't forget to keep this analysis in mind. You may want to use different mediums or intervals to repeat the message. As a result, your power of familiarity will result in approval.

Using Monroe's motivated sequence

There is a time-tested organizing structure, and it is called Monroe's motivated sequence. When you have the intention of persuading with a presentation, you can use it if you want your listeners to do something. Monroe's motivated sequence involves:

Capture the attention

If you want your listeners to pay attention to what you want to say, hook them from the beginning. You have various gambits to accomplish this method, including a brief story, a question or a rhetorical question, a remarkable visual, a startling statistic, and a powerful quote.

Establish the need

Give your listeners the reason to believe that there is a problem that you want to address. Your audience will conclude that they should care when you do this. Your purpose at this point is to make them think that they need to hear this message and perhaps do something about the problem.

Satisfy the need

Your listeners must be aware that you have unique skills or knowledge to fill that need. Let them know that the issue of the problem they may have has a solution which is within your reach.

Visualize the results

Take your listeners through a journey of positive visualization. Help them see the benefits of adopting your proposal or solution.

Make them go through a negative visualization where they will see the consequences of not taking any action. You must know that your main goal here is for your audience to imagine that this is a great idea.

Ask for the action

Then, you must clearly outline the action you want them to take. Here, your goal is for them to decide they want your product or service and desperately by now for you to show them how to get it.

The Difference between Manipulation and Persuasion

Two concepts that are quite related closely are manipulation and persuasion, and occasionally, the thin line connecting the two appears to blur. To have a clear understating of the moment when the crisscrossing to manipulation happens, we have an in-depth look into the meaning of the two words.

With persuasion, we are making people believe or do something. Every day, we engage in persuasion, and there's egotism in the attempt. It is by getting a person to have a rethink about the beliefs that serve them, and change to a perspective that we believe is right.

As one of the various ways of relating to people around us, there's not evil about persuasion. If we have a selfless frame of mind through persuasion means seeing the world becoming a safe place. Even if we want to become wealthy, it is not immoral or evil to make money. You will only have to persuade people they need to spend their money because the people you are trying to convince are looking to keep their money.

Manipulation, on the other hand, use unfair or artful means to serve the purpose of someone. Here, there is no mistake about self-interest since no matter what; you must achieve your desire. Even if there is an advantage to such individual that someone manipulates, that is only an offshoot of the central objective of the person who engages in manipulation. Therefore, three things stand between manipulation and persuasion, and they are:

- The transparency and truthfulness of the method

- The net impact or benefit on the subject

- The purpose that runs desire to persuade a certain person

There is importance to the goal of someone attempting to manipulate or persuasion. With manipulation, the buyer will feel remorse immediately the message is over, while people feel happy to have made contact with you in the case of influence.

The rise of vulnerability

Though trust is perilously low in today's world where the concepts are particularly essential, people need to be mindful of whether they are manipulative or persuasive continually.

Several reasons force us to be susceptible to manipulation. For example, manipulators have become so polished in their system of manipulating people. However, some issues have more connection with the spectators.

As we receive several more messages every day, one significant problem we face is information overload, and consequently, there is a rise of appeal to oversimplification. For more than a decade, politics has taken another dimension. As opposed to the mainstays of news from years ago, sourcing news has moved to social media. As generalization takes on complex issues, we catch memes and slogans.

One can perceive how manipulation penetrates the mix. What's more? Even when several of them may not be what will be most efficient, we have the willingness to snatch at potential solutions since those increased messages have caused us so much anxiety in us.

Chapter 5: Body Language and Nonverbal Communication

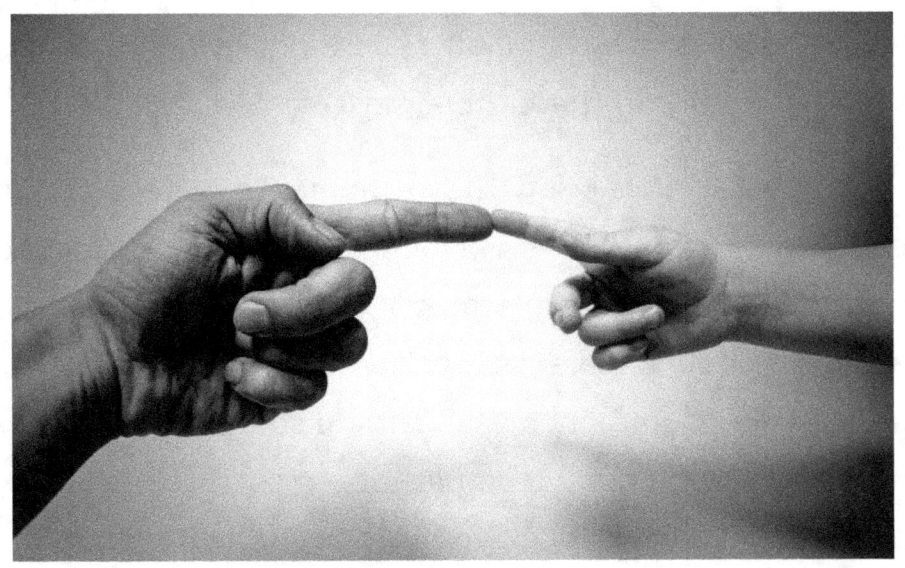

People regularly throw off cues to what they are thinking or feeling even when most of them may not articulate their thoughts verbally. The communication of non-verbal messages happens through facial expression, body movements, vocal volume and tone, and other cues people collectively identify as body language.

As opposed to spoken language, body language is not always clear. However, how we interpret it can make a significant difference in how a person interacts with and relates to others. As micro expressions, it is typical of a silent orchestra such as brief displays of emotion that someone attempts to hide, postures, and hand gestures, even though we are not aware of them, we keep details in the brain almost immediately.

No matter how brief, these moments of recognition can have enduring consequences for how someone interprets other people's mood, openness, motivation, as well as how people around them perceive their inner self. Sadly, some mental health disorders, especially neurodevelopmental; complications such as autism, can make it a bit difficult to react to the body language convey, not to talk of it is more challenging to notice.

Understanding Body Language and Facial Expressions

As nonverbal languages, we use body language to communicate. Experts believe that a massive part of daily communication is the sum of these nonverbal signals. Even when we don't say all these things using facial expression and body language, we pass on plenty of information.

Between 60 to 65 percent of our entire communication uses body language, as some people suggest. While we concentrate on other cues like context, which is also important, it is essential to understand body language. In some cases, rather than paying attention to a single action, you must perceive signals as a group.

If you are making an effort to interpret body language, you should look for the following;

Facial expression

If you can pause and reflect a bit, you will know that with a simple facial expression, someone is capable of conveying so many messages. While it can be an indication of happiness and approval when someone smiles, a frown can depict unhappiness or disapproval. In some situations, our sincere feelings about a specific condition come alive with our facial expression. With the look on your face, people may see otherwise when you respond to a question that you are feeling fine. Facial expression can reveal some emotions, such as:

- Anger
- Happiness
- Surprise

- Sadness
- Excitement
- Fear
- Desire
- Confusion
- Disgust
- Disdain

You can even help determine if you believe or trust what someone is saying with the expression on someone's face. According to a study, a slight smile and a slight raise of the eyebrows is the most trustworthy facial expression. As the researchers further suggested, this expression conveys both confidence and friendliness.

Of all the most global mode of body language is a facial expression, and people throughout the world use the expressions to convey anger, fear, happiness, and sadness.

The support for the universality of different facial expressions is what Paul Ekman, a researcher, found, and they have a connection with particular emotions such as anger, joy, surprise, fear, and sadness.

Humans make opinions about the intelligence of the people founded on their expressions and faces, according to one study. The research discovered that some people are more likely to be intelligent when they have more prominent noses and narrower faces. The research also ascertained that individuals with angry expression might not be as smart as those with joyful expression and smiling face.

The eyes

People frequently refer to the eyes as the windows to the soul because they have the power to reveal a lot of thoughts and feelings of someone. As an essential part of the communication process, it is natural for people to pay attention to the movement of the eye when they engage someone in a conversation. Whether people are averting their gaze or making direct eye contact, if their pupils are dilated, or how much they are blinking, are some of the common things you may notice

Take note of some of these following eye signals if you are attempting to evaluate body language:

Eye gaze:

In a situation when someone is having a conversation with you, and they stare straight into your eyes, it is an indication that they have an interest in what you are saying and are paying attention. Long-lasting eye contact, however, can have a bit of intimidating in it. Frequently looking away or breaking eye contact, in contrast, might indicate that such person is uncomfortable, attempting to conceal their real feelings, or distracted.

Blinking:

It is natural to blink. However, you must also take notice of whether an individual is blinking too little or too much. Most times, when people are feeling uncomfortable or distressed, they blink more rapidly. Occasional blinking can be an indication that someone is intentionally attempting to control the movements of their eye. For instance, because a poker player is trying to appear unexcited on purpose about the hand someone is dealing with him, he might blink less frequently.

Pupil size:

A subtle nonverbal communication signal is pupil size. Sometimes, emotions can cause small changes in pupil size even since the levels of light in the surroundings influence the dilation of the pupil. For example, when someone has an attraction for another person, people may describe the look they give as "bedroom eyes." Another instance is that highly dilated eyes can be a clue that someone is interested or even aroused.

The mouth

To read body language, mouth movements and expressions are also important. For example, when someone chews on the base lip, it may be an indication that the person is experiencing feelings of fear, worry, or insecurity.

When people cover their mouths when they are coughing or yawning, they may be attempting to be polite. However, it also can be an effort to cover up their feeling of displeasure. Perhaps, one of the most excellent signals of body language is smiling, but it is possible to interpret smiles in various ways. People can use a smile to express happiness, cynicism, or even sarcasm or a smile can be genuine. Take note of some of these lip and mouth signals when you are evaluating body language:

Pursed lips:

When someone tightens their lips, it may indicate disapproval, distrust, or distaste.

Lip biting:

Biting the lips might be an indicator of anxiety, worry, or stress.

Covering the mouth:

To display smirks or smiles, some people may cover their mouth to veil a sensitive response.

Turned up or down:

It may be slight signs of their feelings when people have little changes in the mouth. Someone whose mouth is slightly turned may be an indicator that such a person has optimistic or happy feelings. Meanwhile, a somewhat down-turned mouth can indicate disapproval, an outrage grimace, or even sadness.

Gestures

One of the most understandable and direct signals of body language is gestures. While people use their fingers to give signs of numerical amounts, they also use pointing, waving, and they are all quite easy and basic to understand gestures. However, because people have nationalized some gestures, a peace sign or a thumbs-up in one country might indicate a different meaning when you make the same gesture in another country.

Here are a few possible meanings of some common gestures:

- **A clenched fist** may be an indicator of anger in some cases or solidarity in others.

- **A thumbs down and thumbs up** is a signal people use most times to indicate gestures of disapproval and approval.

- **The "okay" gesture** means "all right" or "okay" and people do it when they have the index finger in a circle, and touch the thumb together while proffering the other three fingers. However, people use the same signal to indicate that you are nothing in certain parts of Europe, while it is indeed a vulgar gesture in a few countries around South America.

- **The V sign** indicates victory or peace in some countries, and people create it when they raise the middle and index finger and separate the fingers to make a V-shape. In Australia and the United Kingdom, when the back of the hand is facing outward, the same sign takes on an offensive meaning.

The arms and legs

Crucial for the expression of nonverbal information is arms and legs. An indicator of defensiveness is when someone crosses their arms, and there is a sign of discomfort or dislike with someone when, away from such individual, you cross your legs.

Some other forms of subtle signals maybe when you make an effort to appear more commanding or larger is to expand your arms widely while it may indicate an attempt to withdraw from attention or minimize oneself when you keep the arms close to the body.

Watch out for a few of these signals that the arms and legs may communicate as you make an effort to evaluate the body language of someone:

- **Crossed arms** might be an indicator that someone feels self-protective, closed-off, or defensive.

- **Standing with hands placed on the hips** might indicate that someone is in control or is ready, or the signal may be that of violent behavior.

- **Clasping the hand behind the back** could be an indication of angry, anxious, or even bored feelings.

- **Fidgeting or quickly tapping fingers** might indicate that someone is frustrated, impatient, or tired.

- **Crossing the legs** might be an indicator that someone is lacking privacy or is feeling closed off.

Posture

The way you hold your body can also function as a vital component of body language. In addition to your general physical form, posture is how you hold your body. Posture can express a multiplicity of information about hints about personality traits as well as how someone is feeling, including whether such someone is open, confident, or submissive.

For example, when you sit up straight, it may be a sign that you are paying attention and have your focus at what is happening. On the other hand, when you hunch your body forward while sitting, it may be an indicator that you are indifferent or bored.

Make a careful effort to pay attention to some of the signals that the posture of someone sends when you want to read body language.

- **Open posture** may comprise having the trunk exposed and open. Posture such as this means openness, willingness, and friendliness.

- **Closed posture** is when you hunch forward while you conceal the trunk of the body most times by keeping the arms and legs crossed. When you exhibit this posture, it can indicate unfriendliness, hostility, and anxiety.

Personal space

Have you heard a person talking about their want for personal space? Have you encountered a situation where an individual stands with quite a small space between the two of you, and you begin to feel uncomfortable?

As Edward T. Hall, an anthropologist refers to the term *proxemics* as the distance between people when they interact. The space between people can communicate a great deal of nonverbal information, just like facial expressions and body movements.

As Hall described it, there are four levels of social distance that happen on different occasions:

<u>Intimate distance – 6 to 18 inches:</u>

In most cases, the physical distance of this level is an indicator of greater comfort between people or a closer relationship. Usually, this level of distance happens at some point in intimate contact, including whispering, hugging, or touching.

Personal distance – 1.5 to 4 feet

Between people that are close friends or family members, this level of physical distance happens typically. You will notice the degree of their intimacy in their relationship when you see people standing closer and relating to each other with comfort.

Social distance – 4 to 12 feet

In most situations, people who are acquaintances use this level of physical distance. With people you know quite well, you might feel cozier talking at a closer distance like a co-worker you see several times a week. While a distance of 10 to 12 feet may be appropriate in a condition where you don't know each other quite well, like someone you see once in a while.

Public distance – 12 to 25 feet

Mostly in a situation such as public speaking is where people use this level of physical distance. Typical of a teacher who stands and talks before a classroom full of students is an excellent example of giving a presentation at work.

Mainly, you must note the level of personal distance that you need to feel comfortable. From one culture to another, this case can be different. One oft-cited instance is the difference between people from North America and those from Latin cultures. While people from North America tend to feel more comfortable with more personal distance as they interact, those from Latin countries are at ease standing closer to one another.

The Role of Body Language in Communication

Body language function appears to be complicated. In combination with verbal attributes of communication, body language operates to create nuanced and sometimes a blunt message. There is a role for both the sender and receiver to play, and when they have a different perception or interpretation of their communication; the word between them becomes downright conflicting at best and muddled at worst.

While verbal and nonverbal communication goes hand-in-hand, within the communication process, and over the years, researchers have discovered some fundamental purposes of body language. Some of these roles are:

Regulating

To regulate and pace communication is one of the functions of body language. For example, in a gathering, there are several nonverbal cues that people use to indicate it is the turn of someone else when one person is finished speaking.

Substituting

Sometimes, people use body language in place of verbal communication. A good example is when someone is engrossed in a conversation, and they keep talking for so long that the other person finds it hard to speak up and inform such individual that they don't wish to continue with the discussion. As a substitute, you can step away or glance away.

Conflicting

Fundamentally, it is conflicting when your body language indicates different meaning against your verbal communication. For example, if you tell your supervisor that her appearance was beautiful. However, it is not easy for you to make eye contact while you're making that statement. At this point, there is no correlation between your words and body language. For some people, when the two conflict, they prefer body language over verbal communication.

Accenting/moderating

This aspect of body language enhances verbal communication, or otherwise, it softens, emphasizes, accentuates. It is like putting forth your hand to a child that you are correcting or disciplining or pointing your finger to direct attention to the subject of your words.

Complementing

With some subtle differences, this type of body language is similar to conflicting. You will have a complementing category when you use body language in an attempt to add or support credibility to what you're saying, and people see such body language as genuine. However, it shifts into the category of conflicting when others identify the body language as misleading or fake.

Repeating

People use this body language to reiterate their verbal messages. For example, as a way of repeating the verbal direction, someone might also point to the door if they tell you to open the door.

It is straightforward to separate some examples of communication and body language in ways that you have a clear expression on one particular component or element. However, it is not always precise or clear cut in the real world.

Do you remember when last you shopped around, or as part of teacher/parent conference, or on a date, or attended a wedding ceremony? Do you notice that body language plays a significant power in these entire real-world scenarios and many different ways? Indeed, the best way to become more familiar with the function of body language in communication is to take notice of the cues that communicate louder than words and regularly observe your actions and those of others.

Chapter 6: How to Read Body Language and Basic Science to comprehend it

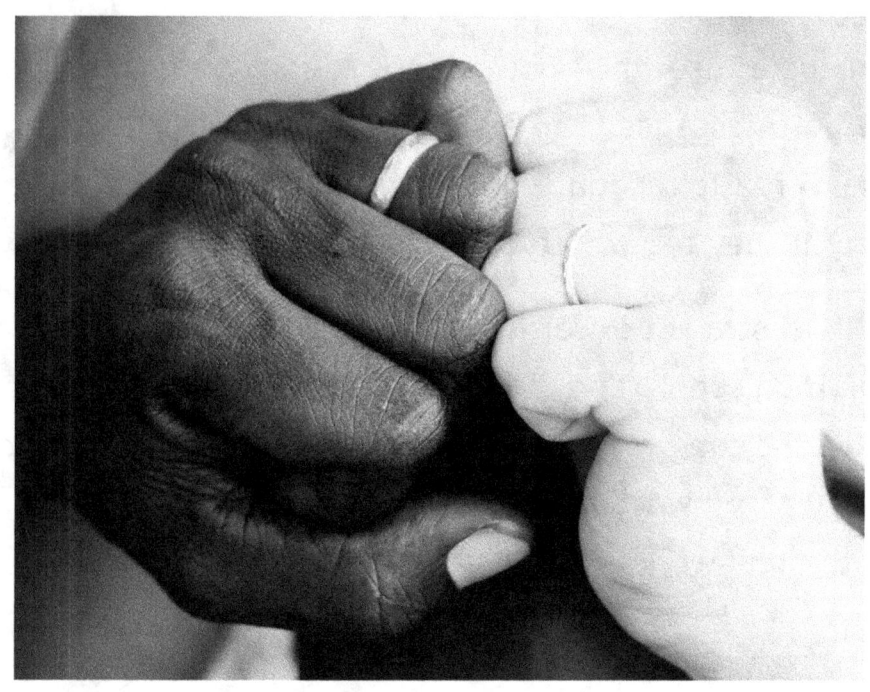

In the last chapter, we have talked a lot about body language and how you can understand the facial expression and body language. This chapter will talk deeply on the basic science of comprehending body language and nonverbal communication.

Having a proper understanding of body language is when you can compare nonverbal signals to the verbal messages that someone delivers after you have observed them.

There are three main ingredients you require to succeed in doing this:

> 1. Nonverbal cues – cues such as body language including intonations and vocal signals.
>
> 2. Verbal messages – words, of course.
>
> 3. The context – let's look at the circumstances or group or the individual in question. What is their age or culture? What is their social status, and are they female or male? These background factors affect our communication in subtle ways and to pay no attention to them is an amateur's mistake.

When you combine these three ingredients, you will get a perfect depiction of the thoughts and mood of the person that you observe. Nowadays, verbal message, which is number 2 in the list above, is the conscious focus of most people. Though people have subconscious analysis and perception of nonverbal communication, they have not entirely disregarded it.

As a result, does an individual component in our communication has any essence? I urge you to read on:

What is the difference between nonverbal and verbal communication?

Become Observant

You must have cultivated sense to analyze and obtain the nonverbal, subtle signals that some people miss or ignore when people consider you intuitive and perceptive. When you have this sense, it will allow you to analyze people's thoughts and emotions as well as social situations in almost a supernatural way. Reading other people come to you naturally, and doing this doesn't mean you are mindful about it.

But what if you are not quite lucky and you can't read body language? Can you guide yourself to become attentive and learn how to read body language? The answer is yes, you can! However, it is not likely you can do it in a blink of an eye; you must prepare yourself to become conscious and alert of your environment. You will guide yourself to sense thoughts and emotions, typical of Spiderman who can perceive danger. We can analyze the process in three steps to do this:

1. Memorize the meaning of some signs after learning them

2. Pull together various clues after you have watched them in action

3. Achieving the right message after careful analysis of everything

In the beginning, it will appear like a deliberate undertaking. The meaning of various postures becomes clear to you but will do you no good if you don't make an effort to prepare yourself to search for these signs. You need to focus on reading people's body language, after you've taken your time, to set up this in your mind, to make it natural and flowing.

Do you know that, by penetrating a process of mindful meditation, you can achieve one of the best ways to read body language effectively? But, wait, meditation? Well, yes. Even when you need to enter quite a clear attentive, and clear state of mind, it doesn't require you to cross your legs or close your eyes. In this state, you must have your focus on the present moment while you clean your mind from any worries, any random thoughts, or plans.

In a short time, you will feel quite peaceful with this fantastic experience and will be familiar with your surroundings. All of a sudden, you will find much more wisdom in the events and people around you, and you will be able to sharpen your sense. Indeed, it is worth the effort even though it takes some attempts to get into it.

Body language in a cluster

Body language is the same as the common verbal language. It is typical of putting single words that you got together to create a sentence that delivers a meaningful message. Nonverbal cues are the ones we substitute for words in body language.

Though individually, these "words" may give us the general idea about the personality or mood of whom we observe, it may be quite hard or wrong to assume anything based on that single clue.

To finish the puzzle, we need additional clues are the things we need to look for to make the sentence complete.

For example, from a male perspective, when you have an impression that a lady you are observing is interested in you. Why would you have such an opinion as a man? Well, attraction and playfulness is the signal that will come to your mind when you observe her toying with her hair? But can you use that single sign to conclude?

The answer is no.

It may not be enough to go all-in even though you might be right with your assumption. Have you studied the person further to consider the gestures she makes and the position of her body? What about sideways glances and whether she is learning forward? Before you decide on the most rational analysis, you must run several questions through your head.

Keep it simple

When you are in a conversation with someone, pay attention to all nonverbal cues, analyze them, and stay focused on the discussion at the same time can be too daunting. The information will not only paralyze you; it will be excessive and burdens you in the end. The key is to let your subconscious mind watch out for the nonverbal communication while you have your conscious focus on the verbal message.

To be a forward-thinking individual, keep it simple. Just relax and learn to be more observant rather than attempting to push yourself to analyze and absorb everything. Instead, be mindful of the present moment and expand your awareness without switching your concentration. When you know the signs to look for and their meanings, sensing and evaluating them will be intuitive for you.

When you have nothing in your mind is the natural and best way to start reading body language. For example, do it when waiting in line, you relax in the park or sit alone. Another alternative is to mute your TV as you watch it. And based on the body language of the actors, make an effort to absorb and analyze what you are watching. To confirm if you understand what you are watching, tune up the volume on occasion.

The words of the speaker and the harmony between the words of the speaker and body language need to be your foremost goal when you are interacting with people. The person may mean what they say, and they may not, but the most important thing is to trust your gut feelings to help you understand. On a certain level, you will sense it, and signs will surface if the person is not right.

Reading body language in its context

Since you are reading body language, you are dealing with people, and they can be quite unpredictable sometimes. That is one crucial lesson you must understand about reading body language. We may get our result wrong in the end even when we assume something based on the previous knowledge we have.

So, how do we minimize the mistake?

The first thing is to be sure you have the right facts. In a country like Bulgaria, we may get into trouble since it is an exact opposite of what we hold that a nod will always mean "yes" nonverbally. The main thing here is to check the manual if you are not sure! As you visit other places with foreign cultures, take time to learn what else this gesture might mean. A foreigner will always be eager to talk about their culture if you ask them. And as they say, there is no shame in asking.

Then, it is time to scrutinize the context after you examined some pointers. Ask some relevant questions;

ask about where you are; the situations and the individual you are observing, and other elements present

Different behaviors are as a result of different settings; since there are various social codes are in play, you must know that a board meeting is not the same as a beach party. You may be wrong if you have a presumption that all the lessons you have learned about body language will be applicable the same way in all situations.

Scientific Body Language Secrets That Will Make You More Successful

If you are like some people, your thoughts may stir towards how you sit, move, or stand. But you should, because when we send some nonverbal signals, others impulsively pick them up.

A more critical rationale to reflect on body language is how science identifies that humans learn and understand their nonverbal signals. How we feel, sit, perform, and the gestures we have is as a result of a particularly remarkable effect.

The fortunate part of it all is it is easy. What you are supposed to be doing is not thinking about using body language all day to your advantage. Rather, all you have to do when you feel you need a bit of boost of creativity, confidence, to feel happier, or creative, is to pick the times.

Use the power of touch when you want to be more earnest

Apart from helping you to make a sale, touch can influence behavior, heighten the odds of compliance, make the individual engaging in the touching appear more friendly and attractive.

For example, in a study, researchers asked the participants to express 12 different emotions when they touch the forearm of other blindfolded volunteers. Without any spoken word, ranging from 43 to 83 percent rate of accuracy, the participants perceived emotions such as fear, anger, sympathy, gratitude, love, and disgust.

Patting someone on the shoulder or upper arm or better still, shaking hands can aid the strengthening of the authenticity of your words when you want to praise someone. When you do this, however small in the life of someone else, you have a difference which will make you feel better and also put the person in high spirit.

Lie down when you want to be more creative and innovative

As Darren Lipnicki, a professor from Australian National University, noted, you can obtain creative breakthroughs when you lie down. He explained that it is when people lie down on their back that their creative thoughts heighten. It is because the chemical noradrenaline could inhibit the creative process, and we release more of it when we are standing. Everyone can now relax, lay back, and try to reflect as an excuse.

Flex muscle if you want to have better determination and willpower

You need blood work at the doctor, and you are nervous when you see the needle. By trying to reduce the pain, it could be that is how your body responds. You need to stay focused, and it will help you when you flex your muscle. Also, you will be able to stand firm from tempting foods intake by flexing. It seems like everyone needs to be flexing now!

Cross your arms if you desire to feel more persistent and determined

We all know, at least we have briefly talked about it before. But do you know that crossing your arms can be a signal to others that you're anxious or closed-minded? That could be a signal of indifferent.

If you want to take healthier action on unresolved problems, you may want to cross your arms. Not only will you perform better, but you will also be able to stick around and resolve the issue. As a trait of prosperous entrepreneurs, persistence is what everyone needs in abundance.

Also, when you feel stressed and anxious, you can cross your arms to help you calm you down. A bit of warning here; do this in your privacy if you don't want other people to pick up on it. Anytime you are in a puzzling situation, try to cross your arms.

Make your best impression of Superman when you want to have more confident

A professor from Harvard, Amy Cuddy, said that your level of confidence would significantly improve with the power posing for two minutes such as holding your arms towards the sky or holding them out, standing tall, putting your hands on your hips while you stand like Superman, or standing tall, will dramatically increase your level of confidence. Strike a pose if you think you will feel nervous, intimidated, or insecure before you make a presentation. Find a secluded place where no one will see you.

Smile if you want to bring down stress

When the brain receives a signal from your facial expression that you are engaging in a complicated chore, it is as a result of negative facial expression, frowning, and grimacing. By releasing cortisol when your body responds, your stress level rises. In a short while, you will be in a tight spot because stress results in more stress.

Here is the cure: smile. Even if the situation is still the same, you will feel less stress when you make yourself smile. Also, there is another cure; there will be little to no stress for people even when you smile, which, as a result, will reduce the level of your stress. So, learn to use one smile to kill two tensions.

Also working out becomes more comfortable when smile. It is natural to grimace when you engage in a heavyweight with reps. But you will discover that it is easy for you to do more reps when you force yourself to smile. Get ready for odd glances at you from others in the gym if you decide to give it a try.

Tilt your head forward if you want to make people, and even yourself, feel more comfortable

While meeting people, it can help eliminate any seeming disparities in status and shows humility and defense when you tilt your head forward slightly. Smiles, tilt your head forward in a slight way, show the person that it is a privilege to meet them, and make eye contact the next time you meet someone.

Naturally, we will reciprocate the gesture when someone showers us with affection. As a result, people will begin to be fond of you if you show them that you are indeed delighted to meet them. Thus, as this gesture will help you to be yourself and help calm your nerves, it will also demonstrate their love for you that they like you.

Mimic their nonverbal expressions if you want to understand better someone else's feelings

Does this sound strange to you? But according to research, you can identify with the emotions other people are experiencing when you imitate their nonverbal expressions. Because of an "afferent feedback mechanism," copying these expressions affect our feelings since we use nonverbal emotions almost all the time.

For example, you will better understand the feelings of someone when you mimic their expressions. Therefore, you will be of great use to the person due to those feelings. Also, there is something we do most times without any thought, which is mimicking the facial expressions of someone else. Doing this creates positive effects on your interaction with them.

Stand at an angle if you want to resolve an interpersonal difference

You will induce confrontation when you stand, facing the other person when the tension is high. And it is even more confrontational when standing face to face more closely. Attempt to shift your feet slight once you understand what your posture could challenge the other person. Walk to one side and sit or stand.

And if someone confronts you, don't back away. Create a slight angle by shifting to one side. Make an unpleasant discussion feel less antagonistic by trimming down any seeming confrontation.

Use your hands if you need to enhance information retention

According to a study, children may not have so much impact on improving their learning when the teacher demands that they only speak while learning. However, they will preserve the wisdom they acquire when requiring them to gesture.

This instance can work for adults since this works for children, too. A researcher said that the fundamental function in education is to gesture, and it is a personified way of symbolizing fresh initiatives when you give learners an option.

Chew gum if you want to feel more upbeat and happier

Granted, it may not appear trained to munch on a wad of gum. Still, several studies show that you can be more observant when you chew gum. Also, it can enhance your response times, or sustained and selective attention, as well as your disposition.

Attention here: drop in some gum, cross your arms as you lie down when you want to crack a puzzle. So, go ahead, accomplish your innovation with this fascinating recipe.

Chapter 7: A Comprehensive Look at Covert Emotional Manipulation

Covert emotional manipulation is an exceptional phenomenon that can happen to anybody, even you. Covert emotional manipulation occurs when a person uses dishonest and deceptive schemes to transform your thinking, perceptions, and behavior to gain control and power over you. When you are in a state where you feel less confident, less intelligent, less sane, less reliable, less secure, or less than what you were before, you are covertly emotionally manipulated. Behind the intensity of your mindfulness alertness is where emotional manipulation operates, and restrains you emotionally, while as a victim, you know nothing about what is happening.

Some of what a skillful emotional manipulator will do to you is to influence you to place into their hands all your sensitive safety and senses of self-worth. Manipulators will continually and methodically break off your self-esteem and identity until there is little left the instant you make such a severe miscalculation.

Psychopaths and manipulators manipulate much in the same way as "pick-up artists" and narcissists. As for psychopaths, they have a perception that they are in charge and look down at others as their game to suit their hunting needs. Psychopaths have no compassion, no remorse or guilt, no conscience, and no ability to love. Achieving anything they want, including money, sex, or influence and taking control and power is a game of manipulators. Not only that, but psychopaths also destroy their victims psychologically, emotionally, physically, and spiritually in the course of their actions. They use all tactics to realize their wishes. They will get going to the next conquest after they have won the game, filled with contempt for you and getting bored.

Covert manipulators cannot have a genuine connection even though they are so smart. They have a strategy from the beginning. Apart from that, they are proficient at reading your mind, gaining knowledge of your strengths, weaknesses, dreams, fears, and desires is so easy for them. With an armory of valuable manipulation schemes that they have chosen carefully and personalized only for you, it is not in them to hesitate from using all these against you. They yearn for control and power and will always persist to control you, even if it results in harming you.

At a point when you think your life has got the blessing of a tender bond through the magical excitement has made a comfortable and delightful appearance, it might be that something quite sinister and different is behind it. To conceal their exact strategy and personalities is one of the skills of manipulators. The main goal of these psychopaths is to fool you into trusting that they love and ready to do anything for you so you can confide in them in the course of a frenzied process of passionate illusion. They craft this stage of deep attachment not only to pin you but also make you susceptible to the abuse and manipulation that will ensue.

After a while, demeaning will replace loving. From then on, degrading will follow, and manipulators will confuse, exploit, and diminish your self-worth, self-esteem, and self-respect. To keep you eager to do anything to save the relationship and to let you hold yourself responsible for not cherishing a great relationship and vouching to save the affair no matter what, manipulators will make a pleasant appearance as loving individuals that hook you.

To show your devotion to the relationship, you will be eager to acknowledge sheer morsels. You won't have any thought of talking about your emotions, fears, and needs, which is not the concern of the psychopath and consider unacceptable weaknesses. When things go wrong, you will shift the blame on yourself, analyzing every mood and every word, becoming quite confused about what is happening, and recalling the conversations. Not only your life or job will suffer, but also your dealings with other people, and your mental and physical health.

Your manipulator will try to have you with them waiting for the time you become a hopeless disaster. At that point, they will let you know with seething contempt and disdain, how they are bored with you and don't want you anymore. Then, they will leave you a sensitive mess who wonders just what happened to your life, speculating your perfect affair crumbled into the gulf of hell from heaven-on-earth.

Struggling with feelings of acute emotional grief and confusion is what comes to all preys of this deceptive and underhanded manipulation. Also, a lot of them experience rage, obsessive thoughts, insomnia, misplaced self-esteem, panic, anxiety, inability to trust, poor health, fear, use of drug or alcohol, and absent of support. Sometimes, extreme and irrational behavior can happen, including withdrawal and isolation from family, friends, and society. Suicidal actions or thoughts are part of what most victims face.

The question is; do these manipulators truthfully want love in the first place? Maybe they never have any desire for love. In a situation such as this, the purpose is that of victimization. The manipulator would have had their plans for their target when they discovered that you are open to their advances.

On the other hand, the occasion might end up badly even if the manipulator has a real attraction for you. The fact is because it is the incentive scheme of the brain, things, and people stimulate and excite these people. Indeed, for those with psychopaths, the system works quite well enough. Indeed, studies have found that far than that of an average individual, the reward system of manipulators is more sensitive. Consequently, it is with the intensity that they establish a relationship.

A Deeper Look at Manipulation Tactics

Covert manipulative individuals make use of tactics to accomplish two things simultaneously:

1. Conceal their intention

2. Invite you to fear, doubt, and concede

Tactics that are generally the most effective in manipulating other people, especially neurotics, are a few tactics covert manipulative people use more frequently. The key to personal empowerment is to know how to deal with these methods of manipulation when you recognize them.

With the use of just about any behavior imaginable to accomplish their aims, it is so amazing how capable the more skilled manipulators can be. Armed with these tactics, manipulators will thoroughly evaluate how they will manipulate the character of their target, when the manipulators know their victim inside out and are familiar with their target's fears, sensitivities, conscientiousness level, core beliefs, and so much more. And in a covert war of dominance, manipulators will have a considerable prospect making way for them to use the traits of that person, especially their most collectively attractive characteristics against them.

It will be appropriate for us to focus our attention of the more conventional approaches they employ and to give in-depth details why the tactics are so efficient because it is not realistic to talk about different feasible behaviors covert manipulators can use to influence another person. Having a good understanding of the fundamentals of the way manipulation works will not only reinforce your insight to the various potential tactics manipulators might apply but also give you superior conscious control of the nature of upsetting encounters with all manipulators.

There is a rationalization tactic which we may call "justifying" or "excuse-making." Originated from the Freudian notion, the word rationalization indicates that, on occasion, against the fear they might have suffered by engaging in dealings that damage their principles, people defend themselves unaware. They will assuage any qualms of conscience when they find reasons that appear to make their achievement more benign, appropriate, understandable, and acceptable. However, the assumption for this situation implies that the person has a highly sensitive conscience. And this type of rationalization is a mostly unconscious process and strictly internal.

Manipulators know what they are doing when they make explanations for their actions in some situations. When this set of people is looking to validate themselves, they certainly have obvious intention in mind. They make use of this approach during the time they know quite well that they plan to do something or have done something most people would regard as wrong. However, manipulators stay determined to do it even when they know it is wrong and how their action negatively represent them. To them, they have permission to do it, such as the situation of the aggressive characters or the case of more self-absorbed individuals, or they may clash against the accepted rules.

One thing most essential to identify is that at the time manipulators are justifying their actions; they are neither unconsciously fending off any anxiety nor defending. Instead, they are actively at war against a set of standard manipulators know society wants them to accept. More importantly, they are also attempting to get your support. As opposed to open defiance, covert manipulative folks have preference for this kind of tactic because it does not only help mask their manipulative goals, and also various revealing parts of their personality, but also concurrently helps them preserve a more positive social image by getting another person to go with the supposed rationality of their actions or have similar perception like them. And when the person accepts their premise with this strategy, the door of wielding the mutual domination and contest of image is opening gradually.

It is not that manipulators don't understand that their actions are wrong or that most people would see them as evil; instead, they hate your negative appraisal of their personality and perhaps end any relationship with them. Also, more importantly, that they should not engage in such behavior again is a notion covert manipulative people don't want to incorporate and allow. Even when at present, they still apply the tactic, they are opposing a standard and holding up the inculcating that standard into their social ethics. It is the visible signal that they are liable to engage in a similar activity in any related situation.

Now, let's us talk about denial, another tactic. Denial is a word that had its origin from the psychology of Freudian. Freud invented it as an unconscious and primitive resistance against intolerable emotional pain. With other tactics such as pretending that they are innocent, manipulators often will use denial. This situation is when someone you have confronted acts as if they know nothing of what you are saying or they pretend in a vain way that they did nothing of which to be guilty or ashamed. At times, they will use faking gullibility and denial with such apparent confidence and intensity that you start to be curious about your sanity and perception. That moment, you start out knowing that you have caught them on the action and one way or another, using this tactic, you begin to wonder if you are making any sense at all. This tactic is quite an efficient one-two manipulation blow!

However, by far the main missiles in the arsenal of any manipulator are the strategy of guilt-tripping and shaming. The fact behind this analysis is that precision defines the high degree of neurotics and cannot stand thinking that their actions are shameful or wrong. As a result, making them believe that what they have done should make them feel ashamed or guilty is the perfect way to control them. Conscientious individuals sometimes attempt to put shame or guilt on their prey with the hope that it will somehow induce modification of their behavior. However, they learn quickly that these strategies prove ineffective on them. For these tactics to function, you will need to acquire a considerable aspiration to be an average person and an equally great sense of wrong and right. In short, since it is a quality lacking in disturbed characters, you need to have intense principles.

Covert Manipulation Victims Mistake Interest for Regard

Most times, victims of covert manipulation marvel how someone they thought love them changed to a wicked person. Things were so different when they meet their other half. To be a part of their life is the desire of the other person. They appeared contented to share their world. They bought them gifts and did quite a lot of activities with them. Their significant others kept telling them they love them with all the things this they did for them. Therefore, why did their relationship change so completely?

The fact is that it doesn't mean someone cares about you when they have their eyes or an exceptional quality in you. Sometimes, it may mean that they hope to possess something of desire to them. It is said that folks who end up exploited often take high regard for great interest. However, that is not true of this case. When someone sees a situation they want to utilize, they can desire you intensely. Maybe you can give them lifestyle and security because you are a stable and financially responsible person. Or perhaps your sheer relationship with them feed their personality because of your physical appeal. It can quite flatter when a person seems to have a strong desire for you. Also, your thought may steer to the fact that they value you more considerably.

Learning the hard way about genuine regard

Everyone would jump into it if loving was that simple? There wouldn't be any necessity to demand it just in the way of every religious head in history. You must know that love is not the same as desire. It takes no effort to desire something because we can see objects of our desire that can please us, and we like it.

And sometimes, with great delight, we pursue our desires.

Since interest is different from regard, abuse victims learn the hard way. Sadly, after they have been mistreated and exploited, then they realize what happened. In the long run, they discover that the reflection of capacity for genuine caring is the real character. True love manifests with the combination of genuineness, empathy, free-self-giving, and openness.

Genuine love – unrestricted positive regard

Authentic love does not happen naturally. However, human hearts are made of it. Unfortunately, to grasp it is quite hard for our minds. As we make an entry, a hostile world awaits. We learn to understand ourselves when we see that it is a world where everyone understands, learning along the way to defend and protect.

The Route to Self-Empowerment

The journey to self-empowerment is straightforward when you steer your focus, energy, time, attention, and energy at where you have power. Knowing about the precise means to accomplish will provide you all of the additional required solutions.

The answer to personal empowerment is truly simple. But it is not easy to accomplish. Though daunting, the road to personal empowerment tends to uncomplicate. The question is; how do you then do it? The simple answer is you need to break off your attempt at managing situations, people, and things over which you naturally have no power. Instead, you need to focus on activities required of you to advance your interest and protect yourself.

You can follow these general rules of empowerment by knowing the personality of an individual with whom you are dealing. What this means is that you have to dig deep, so you unravel any form of disguise in the person and evaluate the patterns of their behavior.

To predispose those patterns of behavior, you need to consider the ways and attitudes of contemplating about things. People will talk to you about all kinds of things. It is cheap to talk, and it is most times dishonest.

There are tactics people usually bring into play to control and manipulate others; you need to learn how to identify them. To look good that they are doing so, people engage in these tactics to have their way. Don't give in to these tactics to govern your behavior. Instead, you need to allow your actions to be the guide for your integrity. Where you have ultimate power is when you learn to take firm measure on your behalf.

Chapter 8: Secret Codes of Psychological and Emotional Manipulation

Never ignore the warning signs of manipulation.

When a person's behavior intends to revise the attitude of someone else through the use of deceptive, devious, or even abuse means is psychological and emotional manipulation. In the event where you discover the behavior of someone to be harmful to you and invariably happen to be the one apologizing to them, such a person might have emotionally manipulated you and the situation. And when a person decides to help you only for them to sigh or whine about it so much that you instantly want to reject the offer, then, someone is controlling you psychologically.

The truth of the matter is, from time to time, every one of us engages in some form of manipulative behavior, however, when it becomes the conventional way in which one interacts with other, then, that person is an emotional manipulator. And like we discussed in the earlier chapter, manipulation differs from persuasion. Having the chance to decide on your reaction to a particular situation is persuasion, while manipulation is all about one's "right" choice; the manipulator's choice. And if you refuse to choose, there will be severe consequences.

Individuals that have the highest vulnerability to manipulation are generally conscientious, generous, naïve, or honest people who are unable to make their decision due to self-confidence. A therapist of family and marriage, George James, noted, the possibility that someone is manipulating you is in some clear emotional cues that should draw the attention of anyone.

While it may appear impossible for us to fiddle with the lifestyle of someone else, we have the opportunity of responding to their actions. You can minimize the effects of manipulation by creating stronger boundaries if you discover that there is consistency in some cases whereby someone is manipulating you. Also, your self-confidence will get a boost when you do this. Though, when some people are attempting to use their manipulative tactics on you setting boundaries is manipulative, but it is not! There's a difference in manipulation and establishing a healthy limit since you will set yourself free from your attachment to the outcome when you set the boundaries. Apart from helping you to protect yourself when you set boundaries, it will also give you the confidence to tell directly to your partners when their behaviors are unacceptable to you. Ultimately, you may need to reevaluate your affair with your spouse when you discover that it's impossible to define the relationship you have together, as well as ending any connection with the person altogether.

In any case, against the beliefs of manipulators, "no," as a word, is a complete sentence!

Decoding the Emotional and Psychological and Manipulation

When there is an intention of seizing control, power, privileges, and benefits, with the process of undue influence through emotional exploitation and mental distortion is happening, then, psychological and emotional manipulation is taking place.

There is a need to distinguish emotional and psychological manipulation from strong social influence. As a mutual part of positive relationships, strong social impact happens between most people. As for psychological and emotional manipulation, someone uses another person for their benefit. Deliberately, the manipulator exploits the victims and crafts an imbalance of power to serve their agenda.

It is important to note that not all people whose actions in some of the examples below may have a deliberate attempt to manipulate you. Poor habits are some of the problems of certain people. Nevertheless, it is vital to be familiar with these conducts in some cases where your interest, safety, and rights are in danger.

Advantage of home

A manipulative individual may take a firm decision to interact or meet you at a place where they can implement more control and dominance. In this case, you may lack familiarity and ownership such as home, office, car, or other spaces and whereas, the place may be in favor of the manipulators.

Looking for weakness and confirming your baseline by allowing you to speak first

This is the habit of most salespeople when they prospect you. They will have the capacity of evaluating your weaknesses and strengths when they confirm your basic standard or level of behavior or thinking by asking you general and probing questions. With a hidden agenda, this questioning takes place in personal relationships or at the workplace.

Manipulation of facts

Good examples include excuse-making, lying, or being two-faced. Manipulators make use of this method to blame their target for initiating their victimization. Also, this habit is about vital information withholding or strategic disclosure, deformation of the truth, exaggeration, unfair bias of issue, and understatement.

Overwhelm victims with statistics and facts

By assuming to be most knowledgeable or to be the authority in some areas, most people take great pleasure in intellectual harassment. These people manipulate you by enforcing supposed statistics, the information you do not know, and facts. This can occur in financial and sales situations, in negotiations, and professional discussions, relational arguments, social. The purpose of the manipulator is to impose their agenda more persuasively on you by presuming expert power over you. Manipulators engage in this technique on their victims when they want to feel an impression of intellectual supremacy.

Overwhelm victims with red tape and procedures

Some individuals use bureaucracy, including procedures, other roadblocks, paperwork, committees, laws, and by-laws to sustain their power and position, as they make things more difficult for you. They also use this technique to delay-truth seeking and facts finding, evade scrutiny, and hide weaknesses and flaws.

Exhibiting negative emotions by raising voice

As a type of aggressive manipulation, it is the habit of some people to raise their voice. They have the assumption that you will give them what they want by projecting their voice so loud or exhibiting negative emotions. Frequently, strong body language like excited gestures or standing to increase impact blends with strong intonation.

Negative surprises

Some individuals gain a psychological advantage over you by putting you off balance with the use of negative surprises. This can range from impulsive job manipulators cannot prevail and dispense in some way, to balling in a compromise situation. In some way, you have no chance to organize and fight their move when the startling negative information comes without warning. Requesting for an additional concession from you may be one of the tactics of the manipulators to continue working with you.

Giving you little or no time to make decision

This situation is where the manipulators want you to decide before you are ready by putting compelling you. This technique is familiar with sales and negotiation tactics. With the hope that you will 'snap,' when they apply control and tension on you, they have the hope that you will yield to their demands.

Poking at your weakness and disapprove you through the use of cynical humor

Often cloaked as sarcasm or humor, some manipulators enjoy making critical remarks, so you appear less secure and inferior. Some of these cases include many comments ranging from your older model Smartphone, to your appearance, to your credentials and background, to the issue that you were out of breath when you walked in two minutes late. They hope to impose psychological superiority over you when they get you to feel bad by making you look bad.

Criticize and judge you to make you feel incompetent always

This situation is not quite the same as the previous behavior, where they use cynical humor. In this case, they pick on you thoroughly. Through consistent marginalization, dismiss, and ridicule, they keep you unsteady and maintain their superiority. Since no matter how hard you try, you are inadequate and will never be good enough as manipulators deliberately foster the influence that there is always something wrong with you. Most importantly, they have their focus on the disapproving without providing consequential approaches to assist, or the provision of any constructive and genuine solutions.

The silent treatment

In this situation, manipulators presume control by making you hold your horses and intend to place uncertainty and doubt in you when they deliberately refuse to respond to your logical calls, emails, text messages, or other inquiries.

Pretend ignorance

Playing unintelligent is a classic tactic of manipulation. When manipulators pretend as if they do not know their responsibility to you or your desire, they make you toil by making you take on what is their responsibility. This behavior is popular among the children as they use it to manipulate, delay, and stall adults into taking up the work meant for them. When they have an obligation they wish to avoid or something to hide, some adults engage in this tactic as well.

Guilt-baiting

This situation is for unreasonable blaming when manipulators target your soft spot and hold you responsible for their success and happiness, or failures and unhappiness. They target your emotional vulnerability and weakness and coerce you into accepting irrational demands and requests.

Victimhood

Manipulators use this technique to exploit your guilty conscience, goodwill, sense of obligation and duty, or nurturing and protective instinct, for them to extract unreasonable concessions and benefits. Some of the good examples of this behavior are issues that are imagined personal or exaggerated, purposeful weakness to elicit favor and sympathy, imagined or exaggerated health problems, dependency or co-dependency, martyr, powerless, and playing weak.

Control: The Power behind Psychological and Emotional Manipulation

Has it ever happened to you from a close associate or experienced it from your spouse, colleague, your boss, spouse, a family, or friend? Sometimes, a neighbor can even control you!

Within the human race, as a force so dominant, control is a powerful word. Control symbolizes a capacity to influence, dictate, direct, and maneuver. If you take a moment to search for the word "control," you will see synonyms of intimidating terms like authority, sway, command, jurisdiction, mastery, dominance, supremacy, or sovereignty. These synonyms are quite intimidating, particularly if you think someone is controlling you needlessly.

There will be a clash when one person tries to control the other. The practice takes over our potential of choosing our beliefs, values, and actions without interference, feeling the world as we see it, or acting with the use of free will. On the other side, there would be chaos in the world without control. We will not perform our jobs well enough, we wouldn't find the accustomed stability, and our world would be a mess.

And in our daily lives, this type of control is sensible, and we all need it.

However, behaviors that can rob you of every scrap of your personality is the control whereby another person manipulates your emotions and thoughts. The power of this manipulation will be extremely intense that, without your fault, you will begin to experience shame, guilt, lower self-esteem, and pessimistic self-talk. Like we discussed before, you are likely to be in a one-sided and unhealthy relationship if you notice a repeated pattern of this behavior.

The most horrible feelings anyone can have is for someone else to control them. We are people with an intervention toward freedom and self-motivation. In some respects, control cramps our growth and development, learning from decisions we make, and the power to explore the world around us.

Whether personal or professional, relationships can tear apart because of control, make other people resentful and defensive toward the person that controls, and destroy trust. Respect, boundaries, compassion, patience, and understanding must balance control. We can all agree that you would have a better feeling if boundaries, tolerance, and respect would be used by your spouse, boss, or parents to balance control. Control becomes abuse and bondage without these things.

Sometimes, the control appears to be spiritual since it is an influence that rules us far beyond intelligence and logistics. Since that is the reason relationships between employees and even cases of marital violence, the victim has a hard time bending to the will of the person controlling them. In this situation, loss of self-confidence and abandonment panic is most times a crucial reason. Some of the examples of this fear include:

- Loss of camaraderie or friendship
- Loss of employment or opportunity
- Confrontation or argument
- Growth of an inaccuracy complicated social status or reputation
- Loss of basics or essentials for living
- Temporary discomfort or feelings

It is crucial to be able to discover abuse and control. It can sweetly come to you, a bribing way. Below are the patterns of actions that people may exhibit when they want to achieve control of your life:

To keep track of you

Sadly, some people tend to do whatever it takes to keep track of you. Someone who opens the lines of communication by getting in touch with you could do it for their advantage. For example, someone who hooks you up at social media sites or online to check on you and how you're faring, or attempts to email or text you even when they never liked you. Such a person will generally cyber-stalk you. The effort to get in touch with may not be up to 1 to 3 times a year, and your interactions together the person may be irregular. Using you or manipulating, you may be the objective of the person.

How you deal with this situation is to be cautious of things they know about your life. Having boundaries is quite okay for you, but you can't have 100 percent trusts for someone suddenly wants to bond but who didn't like before. No steps or baby steps is all you need to take.

To make friends with you when it is suitable for them

Do you know someone that regard you quite poorly and doesn't care that they are into you, but suddenly start smiling with you, embrace you, and express amusement with you? You must watch out. Indeed, people may start to like you when they can get familiar with you. It is possible, though, for some people who have accepted you before and then reject you in another second, only for them to then accept you the next time since it comes to their understanding that they misjudge you. But there some people that do not misinterpret you. These people don't have any affection for you. But the fault is not necessarily yours!

In such a situation as this, never fully trust anyone who jumps from mean to kind and then kind to mean. Don't even look at it that it is a mood swing because it is far from it. You need to be wary of the things they know about you and learn to keep up solid boundaries. Keep a private life and resist from being an open book.

To micromanage you

This case may be a tough one. This situation happens when someone loans you money, or significant possession, or have you in charge of their affair and then keep close tabs on you. It might occur to you when, within the relationship, a base of respect and trust exists.

What you must do is to examine the relationship if you realize someone doesn't trust you and is eager to allow you to have access to their possession and pretend they have your interest in mind. Think about why they behave that way, and if it will help the situation when you talk about how you feel. Some of these people want to control you since they don't trust you. Without being argumentative, bring up the issues and explain that their attempt at controlling you is unacceptable and you are not comfortable with it.

To "mirror" you as if you're a child

For intention that may be proper, it is the habit of some people to "mirror" the people they care about and love. For example, in a tender relationship, when a wife goes out for shopping, a husband may monitor her. Because he is concerned about her, the husband may text or calls the wife to check how her shopping is going. However, there's a problem that one must not ignore when someone tries to control what you are doing at a point, the extent of your departure, and where you are that you feel demeaned, suffocated, or humiliated.

Sit the person down and talk to them is what you must do in this case. Avoid any emotion of anger, frustration, or judgmental when you tell them how and why you are not comfortable with their behavior. Never ignite an accidental fire. Go about it with a calm expression about your feelings. Then, if the same pattern of behavior continues, you may have to consider if their practice of controlling will increase later on or if the relationship is worth it at all.

How Manipulators Use Language to Dominate

As varied as they are exhausting, as a form of emotional abuse and mental exploitation, the signs of emotional and psychological manipulation in communication and language that require all of us to identify. Some of the good examples have been discussed earlier in this book including the use of sarcasm, not answering, saying that it is impossible to talk to you, talking down to you, as well as giving threats and ultimatums.

The liaison officer between Nazi Germany and the Italian government, Licio Gelli, the Italian financial, was known for his role in the scandal of Banco Ambrosiano and being the Venerable Master of clandestine lodge Propaganda Due that they revealed out in 1981. Many Italian scholars have written about him as neo-fascist specialized in some form of manipulating the people. Gelli once noted that by knowing how to communicate, you could have control over an individual. His mantra is that to dominate people, language is a weapon anyone can use perversely. And as Goerge Orwell posits, the power of thought can corrupt language, as well as the power of language, can damage human relationships.

We all know this fact quite clearly. There is the almost constant use of manipulation to influence human decisions, control us, and seduce us in the grand universe of mass media, in the circle of politics, and advertising. However, all things become a little more complicated and sibylline when we come to the private sphere.

We exchange words with our friends, families, and partners in this aspect. Apparent all around us are the signs of emotional and psychological and manipulation, yet those that use the tactics most times disguise it.

Also, out of our consciousness, we use it subconsciously. Therefore, it is vital to know how to react to those tactics when you detect them. We must have a clear grasp that not only is it essential for us to watch out of our expression but also the manner of the expression.

An imbalance in the relationship in question is what happens when we refer to the idea of emotional and psychological manipulation through words. Manipulators use language to benefit themselves. Also, they have the goal of hurting you while they use it to control you. What creates this covert aggression inside us is our base emotions.

Chapter 9: Emotional Manipulation Tactics Manipulators Use to Win and Confuse You

The superior wisdom of knowing your enemy is a crucial advice everyone must take when dealing with a manipulator. The insight allows you to have a strategic response to issues. For some people, the manner of their reaction escalates abuse, thereby retreating and taking in unacceptable behavior, falling into the trap of the abuser which makes them feel guilty, small, and doubtful of self. When you learn what they are up to, you will be able to empower yourself.

Covert aggression is what appears defensive or passive when someone behaves violently. To what degree manipulators' behavior is unconscious or conscious is controversial. As for the victim, the situation has no significance because the impact is similar. They will be in jeopardy of mistreating them continually when they are overtly-empathic. When a person gives you covert or overt attack, they are aggressive.

As George Simon, a psychologist, argues, covert manipulators do and say things to accomplish their mission, which is to have control and power. As for narcissists, people with borderline personality disorders, and sociopaths, Simon argues tactics of these individuals are not inherent in the pattern that defense mechanisms work usually. The behavior of this set of individuals becomes reflexive that over time, it is so frequent. Without thinking about it, they are nonetheless mindful of it even without thinking about it.

Manipulator's Ambitions

Needless to reiterate this, for achieving their aims, the purpose of all manipulators is to gain influence, but it is for control and power through abusive and deceptive techniques for habitual manipulators. They sustain control through recurring, continuous emotional manipulation, coercive control, and abuse. They are passive-aggressive most of the time. In their attempt to behave unacceptably and deflect any criticism, manipulators may act or lie or surprised by your complaints, or hurt. For manipulators to maintain power and carry out their wishes, they aim;

- To avoid responsibility

- To make you question your perceptions and even yourself

- To prevent any form of confrontation from you

- To continue with their behavior

- To conceal their aggressive intent

- To put you on the defensive

Ultimately, you may not have trust in yourself, your perceptions, and feelings because they have victimized you. Overt aggression may be part of manipulation such as narcissist abuse, subtle forms of emotional abuse, and criticism. Manipulators have preference weapons of violence including bribery, blame, mind games, undermining, assumptions, reversals, evasiveness, emotional blackmail, inattention, forgetting, apologies, fake concern, favors and gifts, and sympathy. Below are some of the tactics manipulators use to confuse their victims:

Lying

Sometimes, habitual liars engage in their act when it is pointless. They are not lying because they are guilty or afraid, but to convince you to obey their orders. Through some manipulative tactics like accusations, many of these people plant you on the criminal side at the same time. Also, through omission of material information and vagueness, lying may be indirect even when their submission is far from being true. For example, a trickster in a relationship would never admit to an adulterous rendezvous, and they might say they are at the gym or working late.

Denial

Because it is unconscious, this type of denial is typical of not realizing that you have an addiction, someone has abused you, are running away from the truths. Rejection knowledge of behaviors, agreements, and promises is what conscious denial all about. Also, it is a form of rationalization, excuses, and minimization. They downsize and justify their actions or act as if you're taking things too far for nothing to win your pity or make you question your actions.

Avoidance

Manipulators will always avoid any situation where you want them to take responsibility for their action when you confront them. Manipulators may refuse to discuss their behavior and evade conversations about it. A situation like this may combine an act of violence, including accusing you of always nagging and you're on the suspicious side which fills you with guilt, blames, or shame. The state of avoidance can take a discreet and subtle level when a manipulator changes the topic. They may camouflage the subject with compliments, boasting, or remarks that are good to your ears such as asking you to disregard the reason for your annoyance in the first place or telling you about their concern for you. To blur the facts, plant doubts, and confuse you, another tactic they use is the avoidance of vagueness. When you are positive about a relationship, you enter into denial yourself and give someone the benefit of the doubt. Count on them when you have doubts!

Guilt, shame, and blame

A defense where the manipulators accuse you of their behavior, these tactics involve projection. They believe that excellent protection is the best defense. The distressed one is now on the defensive when manipulators swing guilt. While their victims now feel shame and guilt, they perpetrate them freely and remain above suspicion. Manipulators are known to condemn anyone or perhaps their victims. Typically, they criticize their addiction on others, their 'bitchy' spouse or needy boss. Without any defense, a defendant of crime will show aggression on the police or their technique of gathering facts. Attacking their victim's reputation is one of the habits of rapists. In cases of marital violence, the husband who had beaten his wife blamed her for beating her. Shifting the focus of shaming and guilt-tripping onto you will make the abuse feel greater while it makes you grow weaker. When martyrs express criticism that you are ungrateful and selfish and imply or say after all they have done for you, they are engaging in the use of guilt.

To make you feel that you are not enough, shaming goes beyond guilt. Not just your actions, shaming debases your traits, your role, or you as a person. Manipulators will tell you that if the children had a father who knows how to make a decent living or has specialization in parenting, the children would behave. Their comparison is a strong form of shaming, yet it is subtle. It can be damaging when parents make a comparison of siblings with playmates or even with each other. To make their mate feel inferior and have the upper hand, some partners make a comparison of their ex to their mate. Blaming the aggrieved person is part of the shaming and guilt. For example, you may discover proof on your spouse's phone that they are flirting. It is likely for your partner to act outrage that you are taking their things behind them. Now, they have succeeded in switching the focus on you. Your spouse avoids the flirting confrontation by playing the victim, which they can lie about, circumvented, or minimized altogether. You don't want to challenge any rationalized rage and feel guilty for your action even as the real casualty, thereby tolerate the flirting, and it continues without dealing with it.

One particular indication of toxicity is when someone applies all tactics to evade any form of responsibility and frequently reluctant to see their inadequacies. Manipulators are making use of projection in this case. By laying them at another person's door, the tactic is a defensive mechanism to displace responsibility of their negative characteristics and behavior. As a detour, the mode of this tactic is to avoid accountability and ownership.

As Dr. Martines-Lewi, a Narcissistic Personality clinical expert once noted, to some degree, everybody use projection; however, most times, it is perceptively abusive for narcissists. In such a way that is excessively cruel and painful, malignant sociopaths and narcissists choose to put their persona on their gullible suspects, instead of acknowledging their imperfections, wrongdoings, and flaws. They have a preference for their victims to feel ashamed of themselves and accountable for their conducts rather than coming clean that it may be to have self-improvement. This way, narcissists succeed in projecting their toxic shame onto someone else.

For instance, someone may indict their spouse of fibbing even when they are lying pathologically; to portray them as the needy ones, a dependent mate may identify their partner clingy; in an attempt to get away from the reality of their efficiency, a discourteous worker may describe their superior inefficient. Playing the blame-shifting game is what narcissistic abusers enjoy playing. Their objective for playing the game is that you lose, they win, and the blame for their behavior is on you or the larger world. While you are plunged into an ocean of self-doubt when this happens, you end up taking care of their weak ego.

As for those narcissists on the other side of the scale, they usually don't care about change or self-insight. For you to validate your identity and concentrate on the actuality of events, it is vital to terminate all relations and cut bonds with toxic people quickly. Another person's cesspool of dysfunction doesn't have to be your burden.

Intimidation

Intimidation can be subtle without being always direct threats. Manipulators achieve intimidation with a tone or look and telling you that no one is irreplaceable, or they always get their way, or the grass is not any greener, or if you have thought of the consequences of your choice. Narrating a story designed to incite fright is another strategy of intimidation by manipulators by saying that a woman lost everything, including their kids and her husband when she left the husband. Or it could be that one time, they almost killed a guy or boasts that they fight to win.

Playing the victim

Playing the victim tactic is quite not the same as blaming the victim. Instead of blaming you, they will play the victim tactics to arouse your sympathy and guilt so you will give in to their agenda. They will tell you that they are confused if you don't get your support. Most times, if you attempt to discontinue the relationship, more disordered personalities make threats of killing themselves. Also, playing the victim takes place when the manipulator tells you that you have no concern for them, or why you should treat them like that, or no one helps them.

Nonsensical conversations from hell

Don't think you will ever engage in a polite conversation with a manipulator because if you do, you will only get circular conversation, word salad, gaslighting and projection, and ad hominem disagreements to get you off track and disorient you. If you make any attempt to challenge or disagree with them at all, manipulators will do everything to confuse, frustrate, and discredit, thereby putting you at fault for being someone with genuine feelings and thoughts that might be different from theirs and distracting you from the main problem. For them, if you happen to subsist, you are the obstacle.

Have you been in a situation where you wonder how the squabble even starts at all when you argue with someone for a few moments? Well, that is a toxic narcissist. When you disagree with them about their ridiculous assertion that the ocean is green, then, prepare to have your family, childhood, friends, lifestyle, and career choices under attack. It results in a manipulative injury for them because your disagreement has grasped their bogus confidence as the omniscient and omnipotent, it results in a manipulative injury for them.

You must watch out for toxic individuals because they may not make a case with you. Essentially, their argument is with themselves while the audience in attendance that witnesses their tiring, lengthy monologues is you. While breathing it, manipulators flourish off the drama. You stock their arsenal anytime your position contradicts their ridiculous assertions. You will have the power to provide yourself with the substantiation that their offensive actions are theirs, not yours when you learn not to feed the manipulators supply. Use your energy on improving your life and as soon as you figure out your relations with them is growing, break it off.

Generalizations and blanket statements

Many of the malignant manipulators are intellectually lazy and therefore, not always masterminds of intellectual. Instead of being cautious to consider several viewpoints carefully, they generalize everything and anything about your thoughts, making blanket statements that regard the several angles in your submissions and don't recognize the distinctions in your claim.

In essence, blanket statements and generalization overthrows skills that have nothing to do with the unsupported schemas, stereotypes, and assumptions of society. Also, to uphold the status quo, manipulators make use of them. The situation where the problem of social justice can turn entirely into obscured is when this form of deviation inflates one perception.

Also, toxic relationships have a bite of these daily micro aggressions. For example, if you make an attempt to mention to a manipulator that you won't tolerate their behavior, instead of dealing with the real problem at hand, most times, they will simplify by telling you that you are easily upset all the time, and you are never satisfied or take to the broad view about your hypersensitivity. At times, you may be oversensitive, but there is a possibility the addict is also cruel and insensitive every time.

The key to taking care of this situation is to stand firm against oversimplifying speeches by comprehending that they are in fact, forms of white and black irrational opinions and hold on to your truth. When manipulators wield blanket statements, they embody the incomplete one of their overinflated sense of self and particular knowledge, and they don't symbolize the entire wealth of experience.

Conscious misrepresenting of feelings and thoughts to the level of absurdity

Your legitimate emotions, life experiences, and differing opinions can get a transformation into the proof of your absurdity and character flaws in the hands of malignant manipulators. To reframe what indeed you are saying, they merge tall tales as a way of making your views appear heinous and absurd. For example, if you attempt to broach your opinions about your feelings with manner a toxic spouse is talking to you, they will use tactics of responding by asking you if they are a bad person or if you are the perfect person, thereby you will see yourself talking. But you haven't done anything than telling them how you feel! This tactic fills you with an impression of shame when you have a go at setting up boundaries and gives them to power to nullify your claim to have emotions and thoughts about their unsuitable manners.

Also, this tactic is a classic form of cognitive alteration and diversion associated with mind reading. Most times, manipulators presume that they have a clear grasp of what you are feeling and thinking. Based on their triggers, instead of stepping back to evaluate the situation mindfully, manipulators regularly presume. Their actions are as a source of their fallacies and delusions, and as a result, no excuse for the harm set off by them. They are notorious in describing you as someone with intents, making you take out of your consciousness, or outlandish viewpoint unconnected to your persona. Even before you have the opportunity of asking them to make a change, manipulators use different tactics to accuse you of thinking them as toxic, and this is also a manner of preventative resistance.

Should the manipulator go on with their accusations against you for saying or doing what you know nothing about, tell the person that you never said that and walk away. When you do this, you have created a solid border in an interaction such as this. Provided that the manipulator can deviate from their conducts and shift the blame, they have made headway to induce you that, for your realistic feedback to them, you should cover yourself in indignity

Also, never give in to derail. Manipulators can pull a switcheroo on you, and you have to exercise the broken record technique of continuing stating the facts without giving in to their distractions. Redirect them by telling them to let the conversation be focused on the real issue. Cut the tie and use your energy on something more positive when you are aware that they are not interested.

The tactics manipulators use to confuse you are exhaustible. They are destructive, and over time, they can traumatize you and your self-worth can be severely damaged. The first step is awareness. If you feel you may need help to see things clearly, learn to write out your conversation and try to identify abuse and all the tactics used. When you learn how not to take the words of the manipulator, you will know how to respond to them.

Chapter 10: How to Tell if You Are Being Emotionally Manipulated

If only you ever figure out what is happening, emotional manipulation can be hidden and delicate. For a while, its influence can be so powerful. Many manipulators are vastly proficient. They are puppet master, according to some experts, and if you can understand the signs, you might turn to a mysterious puppet. As the puppet masters pull your strings here and there, you have to obey their commands. It is possible for you to know something is amiss as a manipulation victim, but it's hard to point to the cause of it. You may want to find out when you suspect someone is manipulating you. Your case may be that, in the past, someone has manipulated you, and nothing will make you face the same situation again.

Sometimes, it can be quite tricky to spot emotional manipulation. We believe that, in the relationship framework, our partner has extreme concern for us. As a result, it is possible for us to ignore some cautious signals. However, there are things you must look out for if your partner's behavior is mischievous.

When a person is manipulating you emotionally, they will criticize and judge your actions in subtle ways. For example, making a mean comment about your choice of friends is typical for manipulators. When someone tells you that they cannot believe you would say that it may also be an emotional manipulation sign. They may be attempting to generate feelings of guilt and embarrassment, pointing out your weaknesses and faults with the use of humor to undermine or shape their confidence. Also, they will strive to chip away at your perception to cause you to feel confused or doubt yourself, the same impact with gaslighting.

On the other hand, you may want to know that it is not difficult for you to tell if someone is manipulating. Indeed, there may be no need to be familiar with the tactics and methods to realize someone is pulling your strings even though it is smart to learn the techniques of covert emotional manipulation. If you want to know whether someone is manipulating you or not, you only need to observe your persona. And it is quite possible someone is manipulating you if you notice some of these signs;

- Your anxiety of losing your love has departed from the delight you have at finding it.

Your relationship kicks off with big dreams, and then, things suddenly change, and you are in a state of confusion as to how things changed as sadness, anxiety, and still, extreme stress replaces your feelings of happiness.

- The condition of your relationship is dependent on your mood.

- Though you are not sure, it is as if you are damaging the relationship.

- A lot of time you are not contented in your affair. However, you don't want to lose it because you are blissful all the time.

- While you are not sure about the reason, the connection with the other person feels quite cumbersome. You likely find yourself telling your friends while talking to them about it that it is just quite complicated or that it is hard to explain.

- The relationship is your obsession. Almost regularly, you are analyzing all aspects of your relationship and at the same time making so much effort to understand it. Every time, you express the state of this situation in your relation to anyone that cares to listen, yet all these attempts are fruitless.

- You ask your spouse all the time if something is wrong. Though it doesn't as if something is wrong, but you are not sure.

- It never occurs to you your position with your spouse, and that makes you continuously nervous and indecisive.

- Most times, you are on the cynical side of your relationship. You discover that your partner misunderstands you, and as a result, you are forced to defend and also explain yourself.

- Conveying negative emotions and thoughts is forbidden and even feels restricted. Consequently, you make an effort to conceal those things. Frustration sets in for you since it's hard to express essential elements.

- It's hard for you to figure out what to do to make your spouse happy. You make several efforts, but you fail at everything.

- You have a sense of lack. Against your feelings before the relationship, you have no joy about yourself. It seems you're less sane, intelligent, less self-assured, less safe, less trusting, and against your past traits, there are so many "less than" in you.

- There's a constantly feeling in you that you are not sufficient enough for your spouse.

- You discover you are always apologizing.

- Most times, there's a sense of guilt in you. There's a persistent feeling for you to patch up the grievance that you believe you've caused. When your partner keeps some distance, you feel you are the cause of it and then blame yourself, and in your confusion, you continue to blame yourself.

- So they don't pull away from you again, you are cautious of your actions, emotions, and word with your partner. Since you keep feelings to build inside you, typical of a volcano, you explode sometimes. This action has never happened to you before. It only worsens your relationship, and you have no power over it.

- You are doing things that violate your limits, values, or boundaries, or you are not comfortable with and want to keep things intact and delight your spouse.

In any relationship, emotional manipulation is deadly, in particular, a loving relationship. Emotional manipulation creates entirely a biased connection, which can cause you to be frantic about clutching any rationale you get from your manipulating partner. Because manipulators want to keep up full power, fights often happen in this kind of scenario when they try to exercise self-control and individuality.

Also, it is sometimes so harsh for the victim of emotional manipulation. You may suffer low self-confidence due to the behavior if you discover your spouse has manipulative practices, thereby begin to doubt your worth.

You will end up losing your power to reason for yourself if you stay in a situation where your partner continually applies control over you. Not only that, in your effort at evading depression, you will always take cues from your partner. The stunting of your emotional growth will eliminate prospects of essential corroboration, and reduce any form of achievement on your part. In return, you will start looking at yourself as being not worthy, consequential, or lovable.

What Do Manipulative People Do Best?

The straightforward and simple answer to that is to cart off your power. Period!

You will have fewer resources and tools to rebuild and develop when you have less power to grow. One of the skills manipulators have is to fragment the foundation of your emotion to make you think you need to bad feelings about initiating the end of the relationship and that you are not as much of a person.

When a person who is meant to support and love you makes you feel guilty or wrong, such a person is most possibly attempting to satisfy their selfish needs. Since their manipulative partners convince them that they always do things wrong, victims of manipulation get extremely tired of this behavior to the extent that they start considering that they are inferior, unintelligent, and even harmful. The worst part is when these manipulative partners go on much longer; it becomes harder for the victims to have a different conviction. Also, to dish out food in the right way is complicated for these victims since their manipulators will criticize them on their technique. Manipulators will micromanage and judge their behaviors to the level where they are miserable.

How and why the manipulators do what they do is the main setback for the victim of emotional manipulation since they don't know exactly. Not only are manipulators exceptionally proficient at word-craft, but also know the exact language to inculcate shame, guilt, and anxiety in their partner. Manipulators know how to cut down the confidence of their victims so they can have a bright and energetic personality and for the victim to call on for answers all the time.

So they can appear "perfect" to them, the goal of a manipulative partner is to transform their victim behave the right way. You may be blond, and they have a preference for a redhead. Eventually, you may become redhead with the prospect of getting their love and attention. Usually, because they don't even identify someone is manipulating them, many victims don't understand their awful feelings. Above all, manipulators often appear as generous and kind to the people outside their relationship. Apart from looking sincerely polite, manipulators behave toward everyone else with respect. As a result, when the victims talk to their acquaintances about the behavior of their partner, their friends may appear shocked, telling the victims that they don't observe anything like that at all and they may even tell the victims that they don't believe them.

Eventually, when all your friends see your spouse as someone who has to contend with your madness and think you are ridiculous, then the manipulators have gotten their victory. Since your family and friends are not living with your manipulators, they are not spectators of the clever bad behaviors manipulators do when you are alone together. It may be unclear to you the conducts of the manipulators because, after all, discussions with them, you know that most times you are upset or guilty.

So, what is the reason for this? Why is this situation happening?

The answer is because when manipulators talk, you "give them your ears" to them. Indeed, you believe every single thing they say since you trust your love with them and that you're precious to them. Thinking you are precious with the hope for proof and praise, manipulators have put a dirty dig on you to the extent that their words are your breath. Because you are sure your partner will soon shower you with sweet words while they embrace you, you hold on to the manipulative relationship longer than it is healthy.

Sadly, after the kindness, love, and understanding, manipulators will often follow up with observation about what you're doing wrong or bad. Later or sooner, it will happen.

The simple fact is manipulators are quite adept at dishing your pleasant compliments. They are geniuses who emotionally engage you by blending kindness, caring, and feeling concerned about you with blame and criticism. For example, manipulators might even inform you they want a solution to a problem they have to induce your empathy and validating your concerns, however, the plan behind this is to make you feel worthless and invalidated. They use this complicated and smart method to reel you in, chew you up, spit you out, and then with the hope, you'll be valuable, they keep you on your heels back to them.

Chapter 11: Winning Friends and Influencing Others with These Tactics to Enhance Self-Esteem

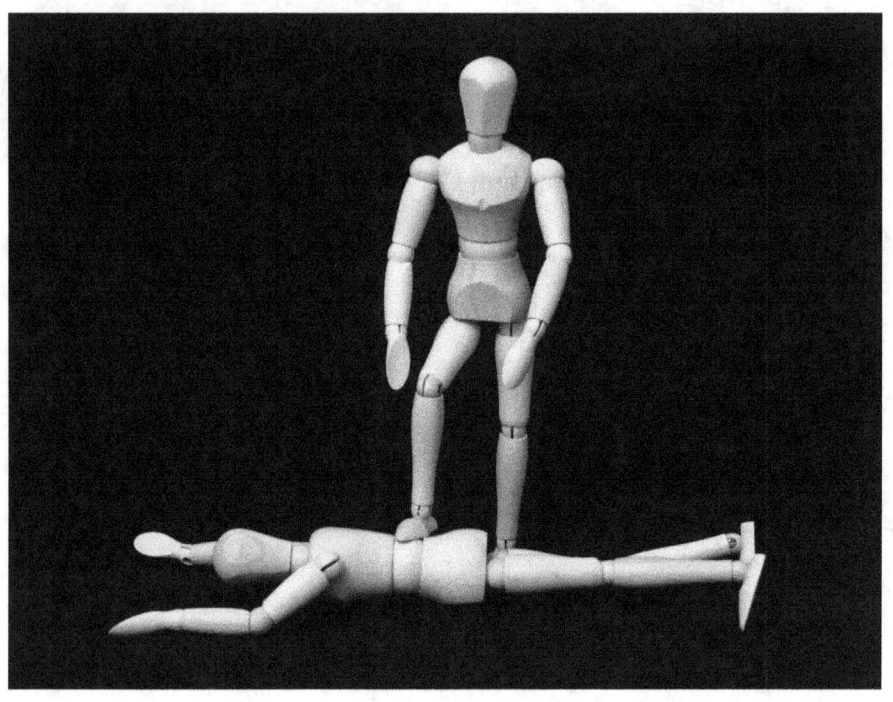

You have made conscious efforts to work out ways to find contentment by evaluating your choices every day and not worrying about the disapproval of other people to have positive thoughts. Ideally, the people close to you would do the same. Though you may not have the capability to transform the way they think and act, you can be an inspiration of positive influence to inspire them to make changes that would result in a more rewarding soul.

Setting a stimulating pattern

Albert Schweitzer, the theologian Noel Peace Prize once said that example is the only thing even if it may not be the main thing to influence people. Rather than listening to what you say, people tend to pay attention to your action. If you have the intention of influencing people positively, you have to engage in your daily life the way you'd expect them to do. You will succeed in inspiring people, at least enough to make changes to improve their experience, when they notice your business success, happy relationships, and additional upbeat life's component.

Value people

People tend to pay attention to your positive actions and word the instant they have a feeling of a queen or king. As Andrew Carnegie notes in "How to Win Friends and Influence People," his classic book; influencing someone is the most effective way to make them feel worthy or essential. Focus on the upright aspect of every person and make efforts to give honest good wishes. People will have the ability to make the best of themselves when you learn to do this.

Project confidence

When you are a confident person, people will want to follow you. Strive not to be a coach of a basketball team who tells his team that he doesn't know whether the odds will be against them or they will take the victory. The team will have no bearing if he tells them this and as a result, they need direction, and maybe a confident player among them will assure them they can win the game no matter what. When you convey a thorough self-assurance statement, you will have the power of setting yourself up like an expert. And as an authority figure, you will have a better stimulus ahead of most people. You will realize how much you can be influential when you tap into the authoritative side of you.

A touch of drama isn't bad

You don't have to turn to a drama king or king, but the wonders of blending theatrical can go a long way in your effort to persuade other people positively. They will always remember when you engage them when something you do is conspicuous. For example, you can add the theatrics to your message when you wear a sou'wester with a T-shirt that has an inscription "love others" and give those at the parks cold soda; it will be hard for people to forget it.

The Art of Winning People

Why you like someone may be hard to say. It could be their razor-sharp wit, their goofy smile, or they are fun to be around. You like them. However, people tend to be a pain in the butt at times. You may have a tough time handling them, and eventually, most of us get angry. But yelling and shouting do no good as it is like exploiting our energies in vain. You can force people to do the job by shouting and yelling, but that will generate a feeling of resentment. So, is it possible to win people and influence them to do some things without stirring up resentment? Below are some simple yet effective rules you can apply in your daily lives. When you do, you will realize how much you influence changes in them without any form of offense.

Sincere appreciation

It is ideal to start with sincere appreciation before you criticize people. When you begin with admiration, it is typical of giving a Novocain before operating. It is important not to offer flattery as sincere appreciation is all that is important. At least everyone has one or two qualities. You have to be the rare individual who can see the good in other people. You need to make the person feel important before you point out the negative parts. This is what the idea of starting with sincere appreciation is all about.

Indirect call of attention to mistakes

It is a great idea to start with sincere appreciation and praise. However, some people add the word 'but' along with it. For example, they may tell someone that they have tried quite hard, *but* the performance is still not satisfactory. You can make a difference by altering the word 'but' with 'and.' For example, you can tell the person that they have tried quite hard, and you hope the unsatisfactory performance will go away soon. Can you see the difference between the two?

Talk about your mistakes as well

Sometimes, we make some mistakes as well. So, why not let the other person know about them before pointing out their mistakes? All you have to do is tell the person that you understand what happened, that you had faced similar mistakes before you were able to work hard to get the result. Tell the person that you want them to know that you expect better results from them.

Never give orders

You need to know that no one likes to take orders. A good leader understands this and makes the team do things, not by giving orders, but by asking questions. An excellent example for that is rather than telling someone to come here and do this thing, as a good leader, all you have to say is – 'Hey there, would it be possible for you to do this thing?' When you ask questions, the other person feels special. The person feels that you care about them and as a result, sincerely complete the work.

Let the other person save face

Rather than putting people down, you need to allow them to save face. So, next time you want to remove someone from a position, avoid telling this; 'We are sorry, but we don't need your services anymore. We hope you have a great future.' Instead, replace it with this; 'You know how useful you have been to the firm. Your services have helped us achieve many deals. We wish to work with you in the future again.'

Praise every little improvement

Do you have any employee who is having difficulties in their work? It may be time you start commending the small details as well. When you do this, it will make them feel special. Great leaders are well aware of the power of sincere appreciation. So, learn to be hearty in your criticism and lavish in your commendation.

Give people an excellent reputation

This idea works on a 9-year-old kid as well. If there is a mess creating, naughty boy in a classroom, the teacher may find it difficult to control his behavior after doing everything. What the teacher can do for the boy is to make him the monitor of the class. The teacher can tell him, 'Boy, you have great leadership skills.' The teacher praises on every minute detail. Guess what will happen? The boy's behavior will improve drastically!

Use encouragement

Using encouragement is quite critical. Rather than criticizing, if you start using encouragement, you will have much better results. Several autistic children have become entirely normal with the use of encouragement. Encouragement gives someone hope. And with hope, the person will move ahead and performs wonderful things. So, next time you see someone performing unsatisfactorily, instead of criticism, use encouragement.

Make others happy about your suggestions

The idea is that someone should feel good about your suggestions. Great leaders understand the rule quite well. They instruct in such a manner that the other person feels responsible for completing the task. The person takes pride in doing the job and sincerely executes it.

Ignite the Art of Reading People through Your Super Senses

If you want to read people, you have to don the garment of a psychiatrist who has the power to interpret cues which are verbal and nonverbal. You need to observe beyond people's masks into their real self. You may not get the entire picture about anybody through logic alone. You have to surrender to their critical forms of information to interpret the essential nonverbal perceptive cues that individuals exude. For you to achieve this feat, you need to be eager to surrender emotional baggage like ego clashes or old resentments and also any preconceptions which can prevent you from making out the person. It is crucial, as well, for you to obtain information without bias and continue to be impartial without twisting it.

In the process of reading a colleague, your boss, or partner for you to understand them accurately, some walls need to come down, and you need to surrender biases. You need to be ready to let go of limiting, old ideas as far as intellect is concerned. Those who read other people well are taught to comprehend the hidden. They have discovered how they will draw on what is called 'super-sense' so they can take a profound observation beyond where you usually steer your focus when you attempt to hack into transformative awareness.

Examine cues of body language

When you are reading the cues of body language, you have to surrender the focus by releasing your struggle to understand the hidden signals of body language. Never get analytical or overtly intense. Stay fluid and relaxed. Observe by sitting back comfortably.

Focus on appearance

When you are reading other people, take note of what they are wearing. Are they putting on well-shined shoes and power suit? The indication for success is when someone deck out decently. For someone wearing a T-shirt and jeans may be an indicator of that person being comfortable with casual. It may be a signal of a seductive choice when someone wears a tight top with cleavage. A pendant like Buddha or cross may indicate spiritual values.

Notice posture

Postures are an essential aspect of reading people. It's a sign of confident when people's head is held high. Or you can get an indication of low self-esteem when they cower, or they walk irresolutely. You can also get a sign of a big ego when they have puffed-out chest and swagger.

Pay attention to physical movements

When you read others, look out for their distance and learning. In general, people bend forward at those they like and keep a distance from others they don't. Also, when people cross their arms and legs, you can see signs of anger, self-protection, or defensiveness. It is an indication that people are hiding something when they hide their hands by placing them in their pockets, laps, or place them behind them. With cuticle picking or lip biting, you will get a sign of people attempting to calm themselves in a difficult circumstance or under pressure.

Read facial expression

Our faces provide the outline for our emotions. Profound frown lines indicate over-thinking or worry. The smile lines of delight are crow's feet; pursed lips is a signal of contempt, anger, or bitterness. While teeth grinding and clenched jaw are indicators of tension.

Take note to your intuition

It is possible to tune into someone ahead of their words and body language. Though not what your head says, what your gut feels is intuition. Instead of logic, intuition is your perception of nonverbal information through images. If you are in the process of understanding a person, their outer trappings are insignificant, and it is only who the person is what counts. To reveal a richer story, intuition gives the power to distinguish beyond the obvious to tell a richer story.

You need to watch out for these checklists cues of intuition:

Respect your gut feelings

Pay attention to voices of your gut, in particular when connecting with someone for the first time, an automatic rejoinder that happens out of impulse. Gut feelings are as a result of if you are tensed up or at ease. As a cardinal response, gut feelings occur in an instant. They are meters of your inner truth that relay to you if you should trust someone.

Goosebumps feelings

Pleasant, intuitive shivers are goosebumps, and they happen when something strikes a chord in us in connection with our resonance to individuals that inspire or move us. Also, goosebumps occur in the course of going through déjà-vu and when you have never met someone before but still recognize them.

Listen to sparkles of insight

During a conversation with people, you may be impressed by those who come quickly. Watch out and stay alert. Or else, you might fail to spot it. For most of us, this crucial awareness is lost because of the inclination to move onto the next idea.

Look for insightful empathy

This cue happens when you have a passionate type of empathy through the feelings of someone's real emotions and symptoms within your body. So, while reading people, take note whether you had pain on your back when it wasn't there before, or if you are upset or depressed following a mind-numbing conference. To determine if empathy is at play, get feedback.

Discern emotional power

The vibe we radiate and the remarkable demonstration of our energy are emotions. It is with an intuition that we procure these emotions. For some people, you will be happy to be around them because they enhance your vitality and mood. Others tend to be draining; get away from them is what you want. Though it is undetectable, you can feel this 'subtle energy' feet or inches from the body. It's called *chi* in Chinese medicine, an essential healthy vitality.

Be aware of the presence of people

Though not substantially similar to our behavior or words, the accustomed energy we discharge is when we sense the presence of the people. It is typical of a rain cloud or the sun that borders around our emotional atmosphere. In the process of reading people, take note of if you get attraction with their presence or retreating due to the willies you are getting.

Watch people's eyes

Humans' eyes convey compelling forces. As the eyes cast off an electromagnetic signal, according to studies, the brain does the same. When you watch people's eyes, you will know if they are tranquil, sexy, mean, angry, or caring. Also, you will have the ability to determine if a person wants intimacy in their eyes or their eyes can give signs that they are comfortable. Even in their eyes, you will know whether they appear to be hiding or guarded.

Observe the feel of a hug, handshake, or touch

Most of us shake emotional energy, similar to an electrical flow during physical contact. You can ask yourself if a hug or handshake feel comfortable, warm, or confident. Or if it is repulsive so much that you wish to withdraw. You can know the sign of anxiety with someone's hand clammy or limp to suggest being timid or non-committal.

Listen to the tone of laugh and voice

Our voice's volume and tone are capable of telling a lot about our emotions. Vibration is as a result of sound frequencies. Notice how people's pitch of voice affects you in the course of reading them. Envisage if the tone is snippy, abrasive, and whiny or if their tone feels soothing.

To read people can be hard sometimes. It takes practice and courage. However, once you are past that, you will gain a significant advantage. Not only will you survive, but you will also thrive in all your relationships with others. People will approach you. Opportunities will come to you. And some people will want to be like you.

Conclusion

Thank you for making it through to the end of *Covert Manipulation: An Introducing Psychology Guide for Beginners – How to Perform Mind Control to Win Friends, to Analyze and Influence People, Learning Persuasion Techniques, & Reading Body Languages*, let's hope it was informative and able to provide you with all of the tools you need to achieve your goals whatever they may be.

Chances are if you have made it to this point, it's because you want to make a change. You desire a turning point in your life where not only can you be independent in making a decision about your life, but you will be on top of any tactics manipulators can use on people.

Imagine how things would be for you if you have in your hand all the tactics manipulators use on their victim, especially with all the practical examples in this book. You will certainly be able to make constructive decisions that will have a positive impact on your life.

Imagine what your life would be if you have a clear understanding of mind control or brainwashing, or how people influence each other. Imagine the power you will wield if you can distinguish between body language and facial expression. And what would it be when you know all about mind game relationships. You will be able to gain control over any situation you face using some practical examples discussed in this book, like being an action taker and how perception is vital in various situations in life.

You have read about control and understand how powerful it is to denote a power to influence. There are examples of behaviors people display when they want to control you. Also, you have had a fair understanding of how manipulators use language to dominate. Life is all about making conscious decisions every day to have positive thoughts. And you can be an inspiration of positive influence when you know the tactics to enhance self-esteem.

www.ingramcontent.com/pod-product-compliance
Lightning Source LLC
Chambersburg PA
CBHW071618080526
44588CB00010B/1181